Assessing the Long-Term Effects of Foster Care

A RESEARCH SYNTHESIS

Thomas P. McDonald
Reva I. Allen
Alex Westerfelt
Irving Piliavin

CWLA Press • Washington, DC

CWLA Press
is an imprint of the Child Welfare League of America

© 1996 by the Child Welfare League of America, Inc.

CHILD WELFARE LEAGUE OF AMERICA, INC.
440 First Street, NW, Third Floor, Washington, DC 20001-2085
Email: books@cwla.org

CURRENT PRINTING (last digit)
10 9 8 7 6 5 4 3 2 1

Cover design by Jennifer R. Geanakos
Text design by Jennifer M. Price

Printed in the United States of America

ISBN # 0–87868–603–7

Library of Congress Cataloging-in-Publication Data
Assessing the long-term effects of foster care : a research synthesis
    / Thomas P. McDonald . . . [et al.].
        p.   cm.
    Includes bibliographical references.
    ISBN 0-87868-603-7 (pbk.)
    1. Foster home care--Research. 2. Children--Institutional care-
-Research. 3. Foster children--Research. I. McDonald, Thomas P.
(Thomas Patrick)
HV873.A83 1996
362.7'33'0973--DC20   96-26102

Contents

WITHDRAWN

Acknowledgments

Support for this project was provided through a grant by the Institute for Research on Poverty, University of Wisconsin, with funds from the office of the Assistant Secretary for Planning and Evaluation, U.S. Department of Health and Human Services, and an award from the New Faculty Research Program, University of Kansas.

Reva Allen acknowledges the assistance of Betty Keller of the Hearnes Learning Resource Center at Missouri Western State College in acquiring articles and documents. She thanks the faculty and students of the School of Social Work Program at Missouri Western State College for their support.

The authors wish to thank Paul Dudenhefer and Liz Uhr for their assistance in editing the final text.

I. Out-of-Home Care and Out-of-Home Care Studies

Chapter 1

Introduction

The history of out-of-home care* services is marked by dramatic shifts in emphasis. These shifts have been primarily a function of the ongoing and inherent tension between the need to assure the safety and well-being of children and the need to recognize and support parental rights and responsibilities. Initially viewed as a more or less permanent solution to the problem of what to do with children whose biological families were unable to provide proper care, long-term out-of-home care came to be seen as a problem in itself. This changing view, coupled with substantial increases in out-of-home placements (particularly in family foster care placements) in the 1960s and 1970s, led to passage of the Adoption Assistance and Child Welfare Act of 1980 (P.L. 96–272), which sought to improve efforts to prevent placement and to move children in out-of-home care into permanent homes expeditiously. These effects have come to be called *permanency planning*.

---

* In this volume, the term *out-of-home care* is used to refer collectively to family foster care and group (or institutional) care. The term *out-of-home care* is not universally employed; some authors continue to use *foster care* as the generic term. Where particular studies use *foster care* and a change to *out-of-home care* would be confusing, we have left the original language intact.

3

In recent years, concern about the fruits of permanency planning has grown, largely as a result of reports of increasing rates of reentry into out-of-home care, and negative outcomes for children returned home; erosion of earlier policy and program commitments to adoptive placements for special-needs children, recognition of the high proportions of adolescents in care who "age out" of the system each year, and evidence of the overrepresentation of children formerly in care among adult populations with problems. These shifting trends in expectations and outcomes of out-of-home care demonstrate how difficult it is to design policies and programs when the goals of child protection and family preservation are in conflict.

This book provides a comprehensive and critical review of the impact of out-of-home care on the children served. Its specific objectives are to:

- provide a framework for the critical assessment of the trends that have evolved in programs and policies;

- identify what is known and what the gaps are in knowledge concerning the impact of out-of-home care;

- develop recommendations for future data collection and research; and

- provide recommendations for program and policy development.

To meet these objectives, the authors reviewed out-of-home care research conducted or published since 1960 to 1992. Chapter 2 gives a brief history of out-of-home care in this country. This historical perspective provides a context for understanding current conflicts in policy and practice.

Chapter 3 describes the conceptual framework that organizes and focuses our search of the out-of-home care literature and the processing of findings. This framework is built on four components.

The first component distinguishes different stages in the out-of-home care system (input, process, output, and outcome) and the relationships between those stages. The second component describes the types of research studies (descriptive, trend analysis, and evaluative).

The third and perhaps most important component of the conceptual framework is its focus on outcomes. This component takes the position that the most important questions to be asked about out-of-home care concern its long-term impact on the children who are part of it. Is a child's ability to function as an adult impaired or enhanced as a result of the time spent in out-of-home care? Adult functioning is divided into four critical outcomes: adult self-sufficiency, behavioral adjustment, family and social support systems, and overall well-being. This focus on outcomes also guides the search through the much larger body of research describing the determinants of placement, experience in placement, and discharge status. From an outcomes perspective, the relevance of these descriptive, input- and process-oriented studies is the identification of factors that might influence long-term outcomes.

The final component of the conceptual framework is an attempt to differentiate the out-of-home care experience along several features, including the type of placement, antecedents to placement, and characteristics of the child. Although the major function of this review is to sort through these differentiating factors to decide which are important, we needed to make some distinctions *a priori* to better focus our study.

An outcomes perspective requires that one start at the end. Only a limited number of studies have looked at the long-term functioning of children formerly in out-of-home care. These studies vary significantly in design, sample size, use of comparison groups, population, and quality. Chapter 4 describes the search strategies used to identify studies, presents an overview of the studies themselves, and critiques the research methodologies they use. A more detailed description of the individual studies is provided in an appendix to this book.

Chapters 5 to 8 (Section III) present the findings from the studies identified in Chapter 4. These chapters are organized around the critical outcomes identified in Chapter 3. Each of these chapters first focuses on reported outcomes, some explicitly utilizing comparisons, some not. Studies of adult populations who fail to function adequately by society's standards (the homeless and those on welfare, for example) are then introduced to determine if children formerly in out-of-home care are, as adults, overrepresented in their ranks. Chapter 5 looks at issues of adult self-sufficiency, including educational attainment and intellectual ability, employment and economic stability, and residential status and housing. Chapter 6 examines adult behavioral adjustment as reflected in reported criminal behavior and chemical dependency. In Chapter 7, results are reported for those studies that looked at family and social adjustment, including marriage and parenting, involvement with the biological and foster families, relationships with peers, and community involvement. Finally, Chapter 8 reports results on overall well-being (mental and emotional health, physical health, and life satisfaction).

Chapters 9 to 11 (Section IV) focus on summarizing the research reviewed in the previous chapters and extrapolating from it. An integration of the outcome findings is provided in Chapter 9, followed in Chapter 10 by the identification of factors that might influence these outcomes. The final chapter returns to the earlier methodological critique of the studies to suggest approaches to the formulation of research and policy that might lead to more definitive answers to questions about the treatment and protection of children whose own families and communities are unable to care for them.

Chapter 2

Out-of-Home Care in the United States: A Brief History

To fully understand the present state of the out-of-home care system requires some appreciation of its origins and evolution. More extensive histories are provided elsewhere (see, for example, Kadushin & Martin [1988]; Laird & Hartman [1985]); the intent here is to provide some background on major developments and shifts in the program's history that help explain current goals and the policies and practices that flow from these goals.

Figure 2.1 provides a timeline that identifies and summarizes some major milestones in the evolution of out-of-home care services in this country. The origins of the current system can be traced to Charles Loring Brace, who established The Placing Out System at the New York Children's Aid Society in 1853. Brace's program was oriented toward *child placement*, with the main goal being the protection of the community rather than the protection of the children being placed. The program involved the placement of eastern, largely urban, vagrant children whose behavior (e.g., violence, robbery, prostitution) the public viewed as a threat. The children were placed in western, largely rural areas of the country. In that era, placement at such distances resulted in a complete severance of the child's ties with family and community of

Figure 2.1

Milestones in the Evolution of Foster Care

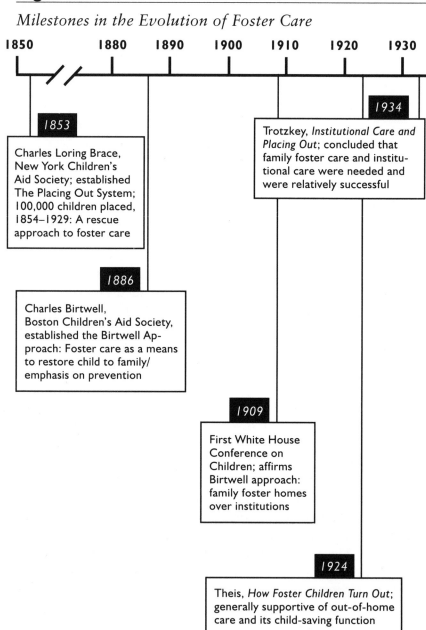

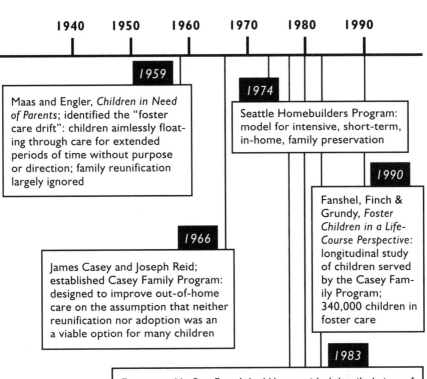

1940   1950   1960   1970   1980   1990

1959
Maas and Engler, *Children in Need of Parents*; identified the "foster care drift": children aimlessly floating through care for extended periods of time without purpose or direction; family reunification largely ignored

1974
Seattle Homebuilders Program: model for intensive, short-term, in-home, family preservation

1990
Fanshel, Finch & Grundy, *Foster Children in a Life-Course Perspective*: longitudinal study of children served by the Casey Family Program; 340,000 children in foster care

1966
James Casey and Joseph Reid; established Casey Family Program: designed to improve out-of-home care on the assumption that neither reunification nor adoption was an a viable option for many children

1983
Festinger, *No One Ever Asked Us*: provided detailed view of certain aspects of the lives of young adults discharged from out-of-home care or reached age of maturity and to obtain the experiences and way to improve out-of-home care; 276,000 children in out-of-home care

1978
Indian Child Welfare Act (P.L. 95–608): increased the authority of tribal courts to determine the placement of community children to deal with the problem of high placement rates of Native American children in non-Native American homes

1980
Adoption Assistance and Child Welfare Act (P.L. 96–272): set placement goals as 1) reunification, 2) adoption, 3) guardianship, and 4) long-term out-of-home care; 303,500 children in out-of-home care

origin. Placements were viewed as more or less permanent, although no formal attempt was made to encourage adoption. The New York Children's Aid Society retained legal custody of the child and could remove the child from the foster home at any time. No attempt was made to work with biological parents toward family reunification, despite the fact that a fair number of the children had one or even two living parents.

The placing-out approach grew and spread. By 1923, Children's Aid Societies had been established in 34 states. An estimated 100,000 children from New York City alone were placed between the years 1854 and 1929 [Kadushin & Martin 1988].

Criticisms of the placing-out system began shortly after its inception. The potential for the mistreatment of the children was obvious to anyone willing to look at the practice from the child's perspective. While anecdotal information was cited, none of these criticisms appear to have been based on any systematic investigation of the outcomes of placement. Accusations by the New York Prison Association in 1876 that midwestern prisons were filled with former wards of Brace's program led Brace to sponsor a series of studies to investigate the allegations. These studies, however, which indicated that only a limited number of children were maltreated or turned out poorly, left "much to be desired in terms of their objectivity, the nature of sampling methods employed, and the somewhat haphazard way in which they were obtained" [Kadushin 1974].

Beginning in 1886, under the leadership of Charles Birtwell, the Boston Children's Aid Society pioneered a new approach to out-of-home care (the Birtwell Approach), one that, in contrast to Brace's program, was much more oriented to the needs of the child and the potential and importance of the biological family. The foster parent-foster child relationship was designed to become "a means through which the child [was] ultimately restored to the family" [Kadushin &

Martin 1988]. The use of preventive services was also stressed to help avoid placement altogether for some children. This approach to out-of-home care gained acceptance over the "rescue" approach of Charles Brace and was affirmed by the First White House Conference on Children in 1909.

The use of institutional placements versus family settings for children has been the subject of debate since the inception of Brace's placing-out family foster care system. With the closing to children at the end of the nineteenth century of mixed almshouses, where all types of dependent populations were housed together, family foster care became the preferred placement alternative. This position was embraced by the 1909 White House Conference on Children.

It is noteworthy that this early shift from institutions to foster families and the increased emphasis on family preservation over child saving were not prompted by systematic study. No significant studies of the effectiveness of out-of-home care were undertaken for some 25 years following publication of the last Brace-sponsored studies [Wolins & Piliavin 1964]. Two significant studies published in 1924 and 1930, however, reported results that did not appear to support these policy and program changes.

How Foster Children Turn Out [Theis 1924] reported results of interviews with approximately two-thirds of a sample of 797 children who at one time had been placed in out-of-home care. This study was generally supportive of out-of-home care and its child-saving function. A 1930 study by Trotzkey addressed the relative merits of family foster care and institutional care. It compared 1,214 children in family foster care with 2,532 children in institutional care, concluding that both types of care were needed and were relatively successful. Thus, given Trotzkey's findings, one could not claim that family foster care was the only appropriate out-of-home placement. Following the studies by Theis and Trotzkey, no other significant research on out-of-home care followed for 25 years [Lindsey 1991b].

The proportion of children in out-of-home care of all kinds appears to have temporarily peaked in the early 1930s. With the passage of the Social Security Act in 1935, the number of children in care declined dramatically. Most of this decline, however, was the result of decreased use of institutional placements. Family foster care levels remained relatively stable until 1960, when they began to rise significantly.

The 1960s and 1970s saw a series of studies that served as an indictment of the out-of-home care program, the earliest and perhaps most influential being Maas and Engler's *Children in Need of Parents* [1959]. These studies (or their interpretations by others) portrayed the out-of-home care system as a kind of limbo or purgatory into which children were cast, never to emerge. One identified problems was *foster care drift*, a term suggesting that children aimlessly floated through care for extended periods of time without purpose or direction. Out-of-home care placement was viewed as unstable by virtue of its open arrangement and by the common practice of moving children from placement to placement. These studies argued that the goal of family reunification was largely ignored, and that with little or no parental visiting occurring in most cases and virtually no services provided to families of origin, family ties were effectively severed with the placement of the child in out-of-home care [Maas & Engler 1959]. Adoption, a chance for a stable home for some children, was not adequately developed as an option, was pursued with only a small proportion of children, and was achieved for even fewer. Out-of-home care, which had for several decades been viewed as a more or less permanent solution for children whose families could not provide adequate care, now came to be viewed as the problem.

This analysis and interpretation of out-of-home care provided impetus for the passage of two major pieces of legislation: the Indian Child Welfare Act of 1978 (P.L. 95–608) and the Adoption Assistance and Child Welfare Act of 1980 (P.L. 96–272). These statutes and their resulting regulations are the major forces shaping out-of-home care programs and services today.

The basic goals of P.L. 95–608 and P.L. 96–272 were to ensure that families were not needlessly broken up and that there would be better monitoring to assure that children were either returned to their original homes or soon placed in alternate, permanent homes. P.L. 95–608 dealt with the specific problem of high placement rates of Native American children in non-Native American homes, by increasing the authority of tribal courts to determine the placement of community children. Under P.L. 96–272, a clear hierarchy of possible outcomes for children in placement was defined. In order of preference, placement goals were set as (1) reunification; (2) adoption; (3) guardianship; and (4) long-term out-of-home care. Out-of-home care was to be used as a temporary placement that was used while plans were made for a permanent solution. In effect, out-of-home care was viewed as the least desirable alternative and perhaps a consequence of the failure to achieve permanent placement.

Following publication of the Maas and Engler study, most members of the child welfare community drew negative conclusions about the potential value of out-of-home care, particularly as an extended placement option. Joseph Reid, executive director of the Child Welfare League of America from 1953 to 1978, and Jim Casey, founder and president of United Parcel Service, however, responded by initiating a program designed to improve out-of-home care rather than redefine its role and reduce its use. The Casey Family Program was founded in 1966 on the assumption that neither return home nor adoption was a viable option for many, if not most, children, and that high quality family foster care was therefore needed for these children.

The Casey Family Program does not differ radically from family foster care services as conventionally practiced throughout the United States, but it does include significant alterations. The program serves "hard-to-place" children who have been in a large number of prior placements. Staff tend to be paid higher-than-average salaries and to have smaller-than-average caseloads. As a consequence, there is less staff turnover than occurs in most agencies. The program has devoted considerable resources to a longitudinal study of the children it serves [Fanshel et al. 1990]; that study is included in the 29 studies of out-of-home care reviewed in Appendix B.

Another prominent follow-up study ran counter to the prevailing negative views of out-of-home care [Festinger 1983]. In her retrospective study, Festinger concluded that there was little evidence to support the bleak prognosis often made for children in out-of-home care and that as young adults, "they are not so different from others their age."

There has always been, and will always be, a tension in the child welfare field between "child saving" and "family preservation." In recent years, the emphasis has shifted from child-saving out-of-home care programs to family preservation, both as a philosophy for child welfare and as a set of formal programs and procedures. Although family preservation goals are clearly articulated under the "reasonable effort" language in P.L. 96–272, funding and specific programs have been slow to follow in the public sector. Major initiatives have been funded by the private sector, with the Homebuilders Program in Seattle serving as a primary model. These programs remain relatively small, however, serving an estimated 5,000 children in total nationwide [Nelson 1990]. Interest in family preservation has grown as these programs have been touted as a solution to the high and rising costs of out-of-home placement. More programs to preserve families are likely to develop, even though some experts have begun to raise questions about the possible detrimental effects of maintaining children in or returning more children to their biological families (see, for example, Barth & Berry [1988]) and recent evaluations have raised serious doubts about the ability of these programs to prevent placement [Schwartz & EuClaire 1985; Yuan 1990].

Following the implementation of P.L. 96–272 in 1980, when the out-of-home care caseload peaked at slightly over 300,000, the number of children in out-of-home care dropped to a low of 276,000 in 1985. Since then the numbers have steadily climbed and in 1993 stood at 445,000 [American Public Welfare Association 1994]. With this growth in caseloads and the strong appeal of family preservation as an alternative, out-of-home care is once again under fire. As we consider new policy and program initiatives, it is particularly critical that we determine what we really know about the out-of-home care experience and its long-term effects on the children served.

II. Methodology

Chapter 3

Conceptual Framework

A crucial though often overlooked step in research reviews is the development of a guiding strategy or conceptual framework. What specific questions is the review trying to address? Is the review intended to be exploratory or is it built around specific testable hypotheses or research questions? In addition to answering these questions, the review strategy should establish criteria for selecting and differentiating studies and specify important parameters of the population or problem being studied that may influence the comparability or external validity of the studies reviewed [Light & Pillemer 1984].

Stages in the Delivery of Out-of-Home Care

This review is based on a conceptual framework that divides the out-of-home care process into four stages: inputs, process, outputs, and outcomes. This general differentiation, commonly used in evaluation and program design, takes on specific meaning within the context of out-of-home care services.

Inputs refer to the contextual and environmental factors that determine the mandate for action, flow of resources, and identification of needs and target populations. Of particular concern in the context of out-of-home care are the numbers of children at risk of placement, placement rates, characteristics of those placed and not placed, and the impact of legislation and regulations. *Process* focuses on what happens to those who enter the system. In the out-of-home care system, process covers type of placement services received, placement stability, time in care, and administrative activities designed to affect the placement experience (e.g., case review).

Although *outputs* can sometimes be difficult to distinguish from *outcomes*, the differentiation is critical. Reunification with biological parents (output) should not be achieved at the expense of the child's basic well-being and subsequent functioning (outcome). While reunification may be justified as a goal on the assumption that children will be better off with their biological parent(s), other motives may influence the decision to reunify (e.g., family preservation, parental rights), and not all families of origin are able or willing to assume their responsibilities. Within the context of out-of-home care services, *outputs* can best be thought of as discharge destinations (i.e., reunification, guardianship, adoption, independent living). *Outcomes* refer to long-term effects, such as out-of-home care recidivism, abuse or neglect recidivism, child development, and later functioning and adjustment as a child, adolescent, and adult. Outcomes, therefore, reflect the impact of the other three stages upon the child in care.

Types of Research Studies

Within each of the four stages described above, the review identifies three types of studies that provide information relevant to a comprehensive assessment of the impact of out-of-home care. These are (1) descriptive studies, (2) trend analyses, and (3) evaluative studies.

Descriptive studies focus on the characteristics of programs and populations and make no attempt to discern trends or causal relationships. *Trend studies* place these descriptors in a time context. *Evaluative studies* are defined broadly for purposes of this review to include correlational studies that attempt to identify determinants of placement, experiences in out-of-home care, discharge status, and subsequent adjustment and functioning.

Focusing on Outcomes of Out-of-Home Care

Data collection activities in social services naturally focus on questions of "Who was served?" and "What services did they receive?" Such input and process questions are important in determining if monies were properly spent [Newman & Turem 1974]. The field has experienced difficulty, however, in integrating data collection around short- and long-term effects of programs and services [Fischer 1976]. These difficulties arise from both conceptual and practical problems. In the first author of this book's consultation work with a state agency attempting to develop an evaluation system for a case review unit, it came as a major revelation to most of the staff that case review should ultimately be judged in terms of its contribution to the achievement of permanent placements for children rather than by the timeliness, content, or number of participants in the reviews. Indeed, a permanent placement itself is of value only in that it contributes to the final outcome—a well-functioning adult. Recall that out-of-home care was once viewed as an outcome, the result of an intervention designed to rescue a child from an abusive or neglectful home and assure his or her continuing safety and long-term out-of-home care was seen as a solution, not a problem [Kadushin & Martin 1988]. The notion of out-of-home care as essentially a planning process or step toward a permanent placement for children is a relatively new one and one with which the field is still struggling [Maluccio et al. 1986].

In addition to conceptual problems that exist in developing an outcome orientation to out-of-home care services, pragmatic obstacles also must be surmounted. Even with a clear understanding of the need to monitor outcomes, obtaining follow-up data on cases discharged months or even years ago can be difficult and costly.

Despite these difficulties, considerable progress has been made as reflected in both the numbers and quality of outcome studies that have been conducted in the social work field [Fischer 1976]. The Adoption Assistance and Child Welfare Act of 1980 (P.L. 96–272) is output—and outcome—oriented in its focus on permanent placements for children. This legislation also embodies the perspective that out-of-home care is a planning process rather than an end-state solution. There would even appear to be some agreement about the use of basic standards and uniformity in outcome measurement emerging in child welfare programs [McDonald et al. 1989]. As will become clear in the review of the studies that follows, however, considerably more attention is still focused on characteristics of children coming into out-of-home care (inputs), the services they receive and time in care (process), and where they go at discharge (outputs) than on what happens to children after they leave the out-of-home care system (outcomes).

Out-of-home care will always retain its child-saving function—providing immediate relief from abuse or neglect—and permanency in the living arrangements is clearly desirable. The efficacy of an out-of-home care placement, however, must ultimately be judged by the long-term impact of that placement on the child's ability to function as an adult. Client and service typologies abound, and lists of child, family, and community characteristics are endless, as are the possible descriptors of the child's experience in care. The position taken here is that the only relevant criterion for sifting through these descriptors is to judge them by their importance in achieving desired outcomes for the children served by the out-of-home care system.

Factors Relating to Adult Outcomes

Part of the purpose of this review is to identify the input, process, and output variables that have been found to be related to outcomes. In attempting to integrate and compare findings from outcome studies, however, it is necessary to have some predetermined criteria that help identify when appropriate comparisons across studies can be made and to determine how a particular study's findings might generalize to other settings and populations. This is especially true with regard to out-of-home care, as there exists a wide range in the types of families and children for whom this intervention is used, as well as in out-of-home care placement and discharge experiences. For example, the effects of out-of-home care would be expected to be minimal in the case of an infant who is voluntarily placed in care for several weeks while awaiting adoption. A sexually abused child removed from the home at age seven who remains in care until age 18 represents an entirely different phenomenon.

These two extreme examples help to identify the relevance of differentiating factors of relevance to this research review. The stages in the delivery of care can be used to organize these differentiating factors. With respect to inputs, we would expect three factors to be of major importance: age at first placement, special needs or disabilities of the child, and reason for out-of-home placement. Time in out-of-home placement and type of placement are expected to be the primary process variables. Outputs are represented by the permanency planning goals available to children in out-of-home care: reunification, adoption, guardianship, and long-term out-of-home care. Currently, reunification and adoption are favored as goals for children; they are expected to provide greater support for young adults than do guardianship and long-term out-of-home care.

The input differentiating factors describe the context in which the out-of-home care experience occurs. Process and output differentiating factors describe significant variations in the out-of-home care experience of children. These differentiating factors serve two functions for this research review. First, they help provide a tighter definition of the topic of study, permitting a prioritization of studies. Applying these differentiating criteria in assessing the impact of out-of-home care, we can say that the primary focus in this review is on the extreme end of the continuum—those children spending significant time in long-term out-of-home care who eventually "age out" of the system. In looking at outcomes for these individuals, one must differentiate the paths by which they came into placement (reason for out-of-home placement) and conditions that may create additional challenges to their long-term adjustment (special needs or disabilities).

Second, the specified differentiating factors serve as hypothesized predictors of outcomes. Subsequent chapters detail the search for evidence supporting or refuting these hypotheses and for alternative differentiating factors.

Chapter 4

Identification and Valuation of Out-of-Home Care Studies

Identification of Research Studies

Light and Pillemer [1984] describe four options for choosing studies for literature reviews: (1) use every available study, (2) stratify by study characteristics, (3) use only published studies, or (4) use a panel of experts. In this review, the first option has been taken. An attempt has been made to include every available outcome study, published and unpublished, whose results have been reported in English. Light and Pillemer describe the advantages of such an approach: it avoids the problem of choosing among studies and it "has scientific merit" when one wants to explore all that is known in a particular area [1984: 32]. Its disadvantages include the need to locate every study, to include studies that are seriously flawed, and to deal with studies that are substantively different from others in the review (e.g., those that were carried out before or after a major change in out-of-home care policy or practice).

Several strategies are used in this review to address these potential disadvantages. The methodology of each study is described briefly and its limitations are discussed. Explicit criteria were developed and are used for judging the methodological adequacy of the studies and their relative merits.

Efforts are made within each chapter to clarify the scope and boundaries of the review and the criteria for differentially weighting the importance of different studies.

Reasonable efforts were made to locate all research studies of out-of-home care outcomes published between 1960 and 1992.* Most relevant citations were found. In some cases, the only information available on a piece of research was the reference made to it in another document; this material is included on a few occasions.

Although most of the studies pertain to out-of-home care in the United States, the review is not limited to this country. Documents have been included from other countries whose out-of-home care delivery systems are considered by the authors of this book to be similar enough to that of the United States for the studies to be relevant and helpful.

Critical Outcomes

Ultimately, out-of-home care must be evaluated according to its long-term effects on its recipients—do we provide children a valuable service when we offer out-of-home care, or do we make a bad situation worse? Although assessment of these effects may begin while the children are in care, eventually it will be necessary to examine the adult lives of children formerly in care, with a particular interest in their ability to function as productive members of their communities. What

---

* Various sources of studies were examined: bibliographical references in books, articles, and reports; the card catalog at the University of Kansas; computer searches of *PsychLit* and *Dissertation Abstracts*; reference materials such as *Social Work Abstracts* and the contents pages of recent journals; and personal contacts with experts in the field. Materials available within the library system of the University of Kansas or from faculty and students of the School of Social Welfare were accessed with relative ease. In addition, many publications were obtained through the library's interlibrary loan services or from the organizations or offices that published the reports.

society asks of families, including foster families, is that they produce adults who are willing and able to live stable, relatively independent, reasonably happy lives and who can make a contribution to society.

Four categories of human functioning are used to assess the quality of a child's life after out-of-home care: (1) adult self-sufficiency, (2) behavioral adjustment, (3) family and social support systems, and (4) sense of well-being. These are ordered in what seem to be the current priorities of Western culture, as revealed in professional and colloquial expressions of concern and allocation of resources. The ordering also has a logical flow that suggests that one's functional level in the first category affects the second, and so on. The specific indicators chosen for review within each category are necessarily limited to what was chosen for study by the various investigators.

Adult self-sufficiency refers to the person's capacity to support himself or herself at a basic level. Included in this classification are accomplishments in education, employment status and economic well-being, and adequacy of housing.

The category of *behavioral adjustment* explores such indications of the degree of personal stability as the use of alcohol and other drugs and criminal behavior.

The level of *family and social support* and functioning is assessed through examinations of marital stability, parenting behavior, involvement with biological and foster families, interactions with peers or friends, and integration into the life of the community. The fourth outcome category explores the general *sense of well-being*, mental and physical health, and satisfaction with life of those who were in out-of-home care as children.

Identified Studies

A limited number of studies have explored the adult lives of children formerly in care. Most of these have focused on people who have left care within the five years prior to the investigation, although some focus on people who have been out of care for more than five years. This review includes several studies that do not actually follow subjects into adulthood but at least report on sample populations in their late teens at the time of the study or follow-up. These studies are most relevant to educational attainment or intellectual ability and have little relevance to long-term adjustments such as marital stability and successful parenting. Most of these studies have been published within the last 15 years.

The 29 studies that are central to the work of this book are described in detail in the appendixes to this book. In these descriptions, an attempt has been made to provide consistent information on factors critical to the internal and external validity of the studies. Not all research, however, is consistent in its reporting of the methodologies employed or characteristics of the samples. Missing information is noted, and the implications are discussed.

Appendix A provides methodological information for each study, describing its sample size, selection criteria, and attrition rate; tracking procedures (retrospective or prospective); basis for comparison; outcome measures; follow-up period; and procedures for collecting data. Because external validity is most affected by the characteristics of the children served and their out-of-home care experience, when available in the original study, information describing the child's age at placement; gender; type of abuse or neglect experienced; presence of any special needs or disabilities; duration of placement; and type of discharge is provided in Appendix B, which describes the individual studies.

Methodological Critique

We found 29 studies conducted since 1960 that report on the situation and functioning of children formerly in care who were in their late teens or early adulthood at the time of the studies. In 22 of these studies, the subjects were 17 or older at follow-up. The other five studies, which look at subjects younger than 17, are primarily useful for their description of characteristics that are likely to affect adult functioning, primarily educational attainment and intellectual ability.*

Of the 29 studies that form the core material for this review, 18 were done in the United States, five in England, three in Scotland, and one each in Australia, France, and Canada. Most of these studies (26) are retrospective. Only 10 employ a comparison group. Four, however, provide significant, comparable descriptive statistics for other groups. Sample sizes vary considerably. Thirteen studies have fewer than 100 subjects in the out-of-home care group; three studies have over 500. Most subjects were in early adulthood (late teens and early twenties) at the time of the study. In two studies, the oldest subjects were in their fifties. The reason for placement, type of placement, and time in care varied significantly across studies. In 10 of the studies, however, subjects had spent most of their adolescent years in placement and had been discharged as independent adults. Most of the studies were designed to look broadly at the effects of out-of-home care and to include multiple outcome measures. Some, however, focused only on one or two outcomes, such as criminal activity, parenting skills, or attitudes. Data collection most often involved face-to-face interviews. Attrition was a significant problem for most studies, particularly the retrospective ones. Nonresponse rates were generally between one-third and one-half.

The number of studies and the high degree of variability among them make comparisons across studies and the integration of findings difficult. Drawing conclusions from the findings is further complicated by the quality of the research and the general lack of comparison data. To impose some order on the studies themselves, we rated the design of each

---

* Two studies did not report ages.

study. Five criteria were considered in judging the adequacy of the study designs and analyses: (1) basis for comparison of outcomes; (2) age of respondents at time of study; (3) sample size; (4) rate of attrition; and (5) date of study. The rationale and categories for each criterion are discussed in the following sections.

Basis for Comparison

Ten of the 29 studies included a comparison group in the study design. The inclusion of a comparison group is, arguably, the most important criterion in determining the utility of a study. While other criteria are important to the internal and external validity of a study, the lack of a basis for comparison makes it virtually impossible to interpret the findings, regardless of how well other aspects of the study were planned and carried out. Many of the studies provide detailed and rich descriptions of the well-being and functioning of children formerly in out-of-home care but provide no basis for assessing whether these observations are "normal" or "exceptional." The use of a comparison group strengthens the research design by providing some basis for comparison.

Defining an appropriate comparison group, however, is not a simple matter. In a rigorous evaluation of the independent effects of out-of-home care, one would like the comparison group to be equivalent to the treatment (out-of-home care) group, with selection to the treatment group determined through a random process. Although none of the studies reviewed here employs random assignment to out-of-home care to generate a control group, there is considerable evidence that actual placement decisions may approximate a random process, or at least a process that cannot be readily defined and predicted on the basis of a child's characteristics [Mech 1970; Fanshel & Shinn 1978; Costin et al. 1991].

There are two major alternatives to placing children in out-of-home care: allowing them to remain with their family of origin or placing them for adoption. These alternatives represent the most frequently used source for comparison groups in the studies reviewed. While logical arguments could be made that children who are placed and remain in out-of-home care for an extended time represent more "severe" cases than abused or neglected children who remain with their families or those who are ultimately adopted, the available evidence is not clear.

It is also possible to provide some statistical control for other factors that could be plausibly linked to the placement decision and that might influence adult outcomes (e.g., type and severity of abuse or neglect, age at placement, gender). The presence of these controls strengthens the design and one's confidence in drawing comparisons.

In the absence of a comparison group, data may be collected from other sources that help interpret the outcomes achieved by former foster children. For example, Festinger's 1983 study uses this approach and provides comparative data from general and specific population surveys. A similar basis for comparison is provided in those studies that utilize standardized tests like the MMPI [Heston et al. 1966] or intelligence tests [Fox & Arcuri 1980; Dumaret 1985].

In scoring the studies in Table 4.1 on this criterion, studies that incorporate a control group are scored "+1." Those without a control group but which make use of some normative data or standardized tests are scored "0," while those providing no basis for comparison are scored "-1."

AGE AT TIME OF STUDY. While the length of time between the out-of-home care experience and the study in itself does not affect the quality of a study, it does determine the usefulness of a study for purposes of this review. Since our primary focus is the adult functioning of children formerly in care, several studies of foster children as children were excluded altogether from this review. Of those included, the ages of the subjects varied significantly. Since some outcomes in late adolescence, like educational level, are highly predictive of future adult functioning and self-sufficiency, studies involving subjects in their late teens were included. They were, however, scored the lowest at "-1." Studies with subjects in their twenties were scored "0," and those with subjects who were 30 or older were scored "+1."

SAMPLE SIZE. Studies should include enough subjects to provide confidence in the point estimates describing attributes of the population (e.g., income level, job status, use of drugs). Comparison studies require large enough samples to achieve reasonable levels of statistical power. Since not all studies included a comparison group, the reviewed studies were compared with respect to the number of out-of-home care subjects only. Also, since attrition was significant in many studies, we considered the final sample size only, excluding dropouts. The cutoffs used were rather arbitrary and reflect the distribution of sample sizes in the studies. Those studies with less than 30 subjects were scored "-1"; those with 30 to 99 subjects were scored "0"; and those studies with 100 or more subjects were scored "+1."

ATTRITION. As noted above, loss of subjects was a major problem for most of the studies. Any nonrandom reduction in sample size can introduce sample bias. The critical issue, however, is not how much reduction occurred, but how respondents differed from nonrespondents. None of the studies adequately addressed this problem. In the absence of more detailed information, we assume that the greater the proportionate reduction in sample size, the greater the possibility that the respondents were not representative of the larger population from which they were drawn. Points on this scale were rather arbitrarily drawn to represent the range of sample-reduction rates observed in the studies. Scoring was as follows: 50% or greater attrition = "-1"; 30% to 49% attrition = "0"; less than 30% = "+1."

DATE OF STUDY. Arguably, studies today of adults who experienced out-of-home care 10 or 20 years ago have little relevance to current out-of-home care programs. This same argument would, of course, apply to prospective longitudinal studies initiated now when these results are reported in 10 or 20 years. The logic of this argument, however, is faulty. It assumes that the program in question is in such a state of flux that future or past programs of the same name bear little resemblance, or that populations served by these programs have changed dramatically. Even if such a state of flux existed, a well-designed longitudinal study could still provide useful information relevant to current programs. The care of children outside their original homes has not shifted dramatically in recent years. Instead, as outlined in the first chapter, the history of out-of-home care in this country has been marked by a gradual evolution and the accommodation of sometimes conflicting goals and values.

One major milestone in the history of the out-of-home care program is relatively recent, however, and should be taken into account in evaluating the usefulness of the identified studies. This event is the enactment of P.L. 96–272, the Adoption Assistance and Child Welfare Act of 1980. This legislation marked a major step in the evolution of out-of-home care programs: no longer was out-of-home care to be considered a relatively permanent solution, but rather as a temporary, planning process leading to permanent placement. Studies published after 1980 are therefore scored highest at "+1;" those in the decade of change leading to P.L. 96–272 (1970 to 1980) scored "0". Studies published before 1970 are scored "-1."

Scores for the 29 studies on each of the five criteria are presented in Table 4.1. This table provides summary information, and permits some direct comparison of the studies. In subsequent chapters, the findings of these studies with respect to each outcome are discussed. The beginning of each section focusing on a specific outcome provides a detailed critique of the specific studies that provides information on

Table 4.1

Judging the Adequacy of Study Designs

STUDY	COMPARISON GROUP	AGE AT TIME OF STUDY	ADEQUACY SAMPLE SIZE	ATTRITION	DATE
McCord et al. [1960]	+	+	-	+	-
Maas [1963]	-	0	-	-	-
Meier [1965]	-	+	0	+	-
Allerhand, Weber, and Haug [1966]	-	-	0	+	-
Ferguson [1966]	0	-	+	+	-
Heston et al. [1966]	+	+	0	+	-
Robins [1966]	+	+	+	+	-
Maas [1969]	-	-	+	+	-
Frommer & O'Shea [1973a; 1973b]	+	0	0	0	0
Palmer [1976]	0	0	+	0	0
Wolkind [1977a; 1977b]	+	0	0	+	0
Fanshel & Shinn [1978]	-	-	+	+	0

Study	1	2	3	4	5
Harari [1980]	− / +	− / −	0	0	−
Fox & Arcuri [1980]	− / +	− / +	− / +	− / −	0
Triseliotis [1980]	− / +	0	0	0	−
Kraus [1981]	− / +	− / +	− / +	0	−
Zimmerman [1982]	− / +	− / −	− / +	0	−
Festinger [1983]	− / +	− / −	− / +	0	0
Frost & Jurich [1983]	− / +	0	0	0	−
Jones & Moses [1984]	− / +	0	− / +	0	−
Rest & Watson [1984]	− / +	− / −	− / −	0	−
Triseliotis & Russell [1984]	− / +	0	0	− / −	+
Dumaret [1985]	− / +	− / +	− / +	− / −	+
Runyan & Gould [1985]	− / +	0	− / −	0	+
Quinton et al. [1986]	− / +	− / +	0	0	+
Fanshel et al. [1990]	− / +	0	− / +	0	−
Barth [1990]	− / +	− / −	0	0	−
Cook et al. [1991]	− / +	− / −	− / −	0	0
Cook [1992]	− / +	?	− / +	− / +	+

Note: +1 = Highest score

that outcome. Since most studies focus on a limited number of outcomes, the number of studies addressing any one outcome is reduced, making the task of interpreting findings across studies somewhat easier.

III. Findings

Overview

Section III presents the findings of the 29 studies dealing with critical outcomes of out-of-home care in two ways. First, the actual outcomes as reported in the studies are described, such as the number of school grades completed by the subjects. Second, the relationships between the outcomes and the variables describing the out-of-home care experience that preceded these outcomes are reviewed (e.g., the correlation between the number of grades completed and the time in care). This "backwards look" provides a vantage point from which the infinite number of variables describing the children who come into out-of-home care and their experience while in the system and immediately upon leaving it can be sorted to determine which factors should demand the attention of policymakers, administrators, service workers, and volunteers. This approach allows the reader to evaluate the general functioning of those who were in out-of-home care, to identify specific characteristics of the children served, and to identify aspects of out-of-home care that contribute to or detract from its effectiveness.

Chapter 5

Adult Self-Sufficiency

Achieving adult self-sufficiency is an expected goal in Western society. The potential role and responsibility of out-of-home care in preparing children (particularly adolescents) for adult self-sufficiency have become more widely recognized in recent years, as can be seen in special state and federal initiatives to provide the transitional services and experiences adolescents in care need to achieve independence [Barth 1990].

This chapter examines three indicators of the potential for and achievement of self-sufficiency: educational attainment, employment status and economic well-being, and housing. Education is generally viewed as a key factor in predicting adult self-sufficiency. Almost all of the reviewed studies of those who were in out-of-home care reveal that the subject' average level of educational attainment is below that of other citizens of comparable age in their state or country. These studies provide information on both the levels of education achieved by the time the children left care and the education they pursued after discharge. In addition, several of the 29 studies include data on the intellectual capabilities and learning problems of those formerly and currently in out-of-home care.

Employment status and economic well-being provide a more direct measure of adult self-sufficiency. Most of the studies identified in this book report employment and financial status. Few, however, provide a basis for comparison that would permit the drawing of conclusions concerning the relative functioning of children formerly in care.

Information on the adequacy of housing and the composition of the subject's household is somewhat sketchier than that available on the other self-sufficiency indicators. Relevant findings, however, are contained in several of the studies: proportions of subjects in various living arrangements, subjects' satisfaction with housing situation, number of changes in residency, and adequacy of physical surroundings.

Several studies of homeless persons include references to portions of the population who have been recipients of out-of-home care. Six of these studies are included and discussed later in this chapter and Appendix C. Such studies are revealing in a different manner than are the out-of-home care outcome reports. They estimate the proportion the total population of the homeless who were formerly in care. It then becomes possible to determine whether those formerly in out-of-home care are overrepresented in the homeless population.

Educational Attainment and Intellectual Ability

Educational Outcomes Achieved
While in Out-of-Home Care

If children do not receive a formal education while they are in out-of-home care, they will leave care ill-equipped to attain adult self-sufficiency. Several studies included in this review provide information regarding educational achievement at the point of discharge from care or while in care; only one, however, uses a comparison group [Dumaret 1985]. The findings of most of the studies providing this information suggest that children enter out-of-home care behind in their educational achievement and do not catch up while in care.

Dumaret's [1985] French study compared subjects raised in adoptive homes with similar subjects raised in family foster homes, and with those provided services in their own homes; all came from disadvantaged families and had been abandoned at some point. Dumaret included three degrees of what he considers to be school failure: slight (repeating a grade); serious (repeating the same grade twice or being placed in a special education class for mentally retarded children within a normal school system); and exclusion from the normal school system, such as placement in an institution for the mentally retarded. Combining all three degrees of failure, he found the following rates of school failure in primary and secondary schools: for adopted subjects, 17.1%; for "mother-reared" subjects, 66.6%; and for subjects in family foster homes or institutions, 100%. The differences between the three groups were significant ($p < .001$), and persisted throughout the children's school years. Among the 21 children in out-of-home care in Dumaret's study, "scholastic success [was] extremely rare": only two completed primary schooling, three obtained technical diplomas, and one earned a professional certificate [1985: 564].

The Westat study found that 66% of the 810 18-year-olds discharged from out-of-home care between July 1, 1987 and June 30, 1988 had not completed high school [Cook et al. 1991]. One-third of the children formerly in care who had been in placement with the Casey Family Project were behind their age-appropriate grade levels when placed, and the same proportion were behind when they left Casey care [Fanshel et al. 1990]. Barth [1990] found that more than half (55%) of the youth aging out of out-of-home care left without a high school degree. Festinger [1983], in her study of children formerly in care in the New York City area, found that at discharge, 35% had not completed high school, 65% had attained a high school degree, and 25.7% had attended college. Barth and Festinger do not provide comparison data at discharge; however, Festinger does provide comparison data for her sample's educational levels at follow-up (see next section). Relevant comparisons at discharge are difficult to make because of varying ages at discharge for the out-of-home care subjects.

Other measures of academic performance indicate that children in out-of-home care, while in school, function at a level that is below average, below their capacity, or both. Allerhand et al. [1966] reported that, of the 33 subjects who were attending school full-time, only one was at the appropriate grade level. Twenty-two of the 41 who were receiving any form of schooling had an average grade of "C" or better. Palmer [1976], in her study of Canadian and English subjects, concluded they were functioning below their full potential. Fanshel and Shinn [1978] reported that most of the children in their study were performing below the normal level for their age at all three of their measurement times. The subjects experienced no improvement while in care.

Sixty-four percent of the children in Fox and Arcuri's [1980] study were in the expected grade for their chronological age. Twenty-one percent were one grade behind, 2% were two grades behind, and 11% attended special education classes; 2% were a grade ahead of the expected level. Contrary to the findings reported in the previous studies, Fox and Arcuri suggested that this pattern is similar to that reported for low-income children in the 1971 National Health Survey of School Achievement.

Educational Outcomes Achieved after Out-of-Home Care

Most of the studies of adults who were in care as children provide information regarding the educational attainment of their subjects as adults and some comparative data. The Scottish studies by Triseliotis [1980], Ferguson [1966], and Triseliotis and Russell [1984] provide a direct comparison for judging the achievements of this population. Triseliotis found that almost all Scottish children who had been placed in family foster care ended their education at the age of 15, which was the age at which they were no longer required to attend school. He indicated that this seemed to be in keeping with the expectations of the foster parents. In another Scottish study, Ferguson [1966] discovered that most of his subjects (85%) left school at age 15. In contrast, Triseliotis and Russell found that 50% of youths who had received care in institutions and 70% of those who had been adopted stayed in school beyond the compulsory age. Thus, the institutionalized and adopted subjects achieved better educational outcomes than did the family foster care subjects.

Five studies compare the educational level attained by their adult subjects with a norm population; all of them find that the level of those formerly in care remained behind. The Westat study [Cook et al. 1991] reported that only 54% of its subjects had completed high school 2.5 to 4 years after discharge. This was considerably below the level for 18- to 24-year-olds in the general population (78%) but comparable to that for those living in poverty (53%). No difference was found in the high school completion rate of young men and young women; however, African Americans and Caucasians were far more likely to complete high school than Latino youths.

The median education for Palmer's [1976] subjects was nine years, compared to 10 years for children in London overall. Zimmerman [1982] reported a median of less than 11 years, which she found low compared with both the general population and minority groups of New Orleans of the same age. Festinger [1983] reported that males formerly in care tended to have completed less education than males nationally, but that for females there were no sizable differences. When compared with residents of New York City only, both males and females formerly in care had completed less education. Also, in all subgroups compared to New York City residents, "whether male or female, whether black, Hispanic, or white, the proportion from foster care with a college degree was smaller" [Festinger 1983: 238]. The median number of years of education for Jones and Moses's [1984] sample was 11.5 years, a full year behind the average for citizens of the same age in West Virginia.

The remainder of the studies that address educational outcomes are descriptive and do not provide comparison data. Relevant census data, however, make some comparisons possible. Taken together, these studies portray adults with out-of-home care experience as lagging behind the general populace in their levels of education.

Four of the five American descriptive studies reported that a majority of their out-of-home care subjects graduated from high school, but that their rates of graduation fall below those of the general populace. Frost and Jurich [1983] reported that 63% of their sample graduated from high school, with 22% still in school working toward their diploma. Census data, however, indicate that in 1980, 80% of the 18- to 24-year-olds in Kansas were high school graduates [U.S. Bureau of the Census, 1980b, Table 66]. Likewise, Jones and Moses [1984] report that 63% of their sample graduated from high school, with about 10% still working towards a diploma. Again, the graduation rates of the general populace are higher, at 72% for the 18- to 24-year-olds in West Virginia in 1980 [U.S. Bureau of the Census, 1980e, Table 66]. Festinger reported at least 66% of her study subjects graduated from high school, but the average for 18- to 24-year-olds in New York in 1980 was 78% [U.S. Bureau of the Census, 1980d, Table 66]. Rest and Watson [1984] report 12 of 13 subjects (92%) having graduated from high school, far higher than the 1980 Illinois average of 76% for 18- to 24-year-olds [U.S. Bureau of the Census, 1980a, Table 66], but this finding is suspect due to Rest and Watson's quite small sample size. Zimmerman [1982] reported that less than half (44%) of her subjects graduated from high school, and 11% of the total only attended special education classes. In contrast, 73% of the 18- to 24-year-olds in Louisiana in 1980 had graduated from high school [U.S. Bureau of the Census, 1980c, Table 66].

These five American studies also reported levels of college education, with anywhere from 8% to 61% of their samples having earned at least some college credits. At the low end of the range are the Jones and Moses subjects, of whom only 7% obtained some college credits and less than 1% graduated. Zimmerman reported that 11% of her subjects had some college hours and 2% had college degrees. Frost and Jurich reported rates of about 6% and 2%. Festinger reported that 34% of her subjects had college credits and 5% had degrees. Finally, Rest and Watson, with their suspect sample size, reported that 61% of their subjects had at least some college credits. By comparison, the Current Population Reports reported that 23% of American 25 to 34 year olds had bachelor degrees in 1987 and an additional 19% had some college credits [U.S. Bureau of the Census, 1990, Table 1]. Thus the subjects in the studies by Jones and Moses, Zimmerman, and Frost and Jurich achieved relatively low levels of college education; the subjects in Festinger's study achieved normal levels of college education; and the subjects in Rest and Watson's study achieved high levels. Rounding out this description of college level education, Barth [1990] reported that 73% of his sample obtained some further training or schooling after exiting out-of-home care. He noted, however, that "only 43 percent of those who had not finished high school at the time of leaving out-of-home care had participated in subsequent education or training" [1990: 426].

Although the educational picture for children in out-of-home care is not entirely bleak, there is cause for alarm. Many of the adult subjects of these studies failed to complete high school, an accomplishment considered basic to attaining self-sufficiency in the United States. In those studies in which the data are given, the proportion of adult subjects who had not earned either a high school diploma or a GED ranged from a low of 8% in Rest and Watson's small sample to a high of 56% found by Zimmerman; in between are a 15% rate for Frost and Jurich's young men and 27% for the Jones and

Moses sample. A further concern of the Zimmerman group is that 30% of her subjects dropped out of school before they reached high school.

Even those who are graduating may not be reaching standards high enough to allow them to compete as adults. Zimmerman reports that 10% of her subjects earned a "D" or "F" average in elementary school, 25% in middle school, and 28% in high school (by which time many of her subjects had dropped out of school). Forty-seven percent had repeated one grade and an additional 20% had repeated more than one; grade repetition was not found to be related to grade-point average or the number of different schools attended. Among the Jones and Moses sample, 41% did fairly well, 14% passed at a minimal level, and 6% failed.

As might be expected, several studies showed that their subjects are more likely to pursue vocational or job training than college degrees. Forty-two percent of the males and 29% of the females studied by Jones and Moses had received some form of vocational or job training, as had 59% of Festinger's subjects, one-third of Zimmerman's cohort, nearly 30% of Harari's [1980] participants, and about 7% of the Frost and Jurich sample. Triseliotis and Russell [1984] reported that 30% of their Scottish adoptees and 20% of those subjects who had been in residential care had earned an educational certificate beyond the level of the American high school diploma (the "Higher" or "A" certificate); the vocational programs in which the subjects participated required two to six years of part-time education. Owing to a lack of appropriate comparison data, it is difficult to interpret these findings accurately. A study in 1987, however, reported that only 2.3% of American 25- to 34-year-olds had earned a degree in vocational training [U.S. Bureau of the Census, 1990, Table 1]. Naturally, participation rates exceed graduation rates, yet the very high participation rates of out-of-home care subjects and the very low graduation rates of the general populace suggest that former foster children are more likely to select vocational training.

Three studies queried adults formerly in care as children regarding their feelings about the education they received while they were in care. Jones and Moses report that 38% of their respondents felt that they had not attained the educational level they had expected or planned to attain; a higher percentage of Festinger's subjects (44%) felt this way, and two-thirds of those studied by Fanshel et al. [1990] expressed regrets about having failed to accomplish more than they did. About one-fourth of the Festinger group felt dissatisfied with the amount of education they received while in care, and 26% reported dissatisfaction with the quality of that education. Although many of the subjects pursued further education or training after discharge from care, only 37% of Festinger's subjects felt that they had been prepared while in care to do so.

Intellectual Ability

Six of the studies described in this chapter reported the IQ levels of current and children formerly in care. Two of the six provided a direct comparison group in the research design. Dumaret's [1985] French study compared five groups of subjects: children who had been adopted and reared in a privileged social environment (A); a sample of their classmates matched for socioeconomic status (A*); children whose mothers originally had planned to place them for adoption but who actually remained in their biological families in a disadvantaged social environment (B); a sample of their classmates matched for socioeconomic status (B*); and children whose mothers originally had planned to place them for adoption but who actually were removed from their homes after a family breakup and were reared in out-of-home care (C). At the time of the IQ testing, the mean ages of the subjects were: A and A*—nine years, three months; B and B*—11 years; and C—eleven years, nine months. Over one-third of the A's (and, therefore, of the A* group) and one B subject were enrolled in private schools; one-third was greater than the national average of French children attending private schools.

Dumaret's highly detailed findings involve multiple comparisons on several IQ and scholastic performance measures. Many comparisons show significant differences, and the consistent pattern is for the A group (adopted/privileged) to outperform the B group (own home/disadvantaged) which, in turn, outperforms the C group (out-of-home care).

Dumaret made several additional observations about the data. First, the scores of the C group (children in out-of-home care) were similar to those found in other studies of children in out-of-home care in France: they had mean IQs in the 80-90 range, with verbal IQs often more than 10 points lower than performance IQs. Second, some of those in the B group may have had a disadvantage on the tests because their mothers came from a bilingual tradition, which could have resulted in the children's having a poorer grasp of the French on the tests. Third, it is probable that the subjects were not randomly distributed among the A, B, and C groups; *a priori* selection probably was involved. Fourth, if the four C subjects with IQs of under 53 are dropped from the analysis, there are no significant differences between the B and C groups. Dumaret suggests that such a modification of the C group would seem reasonable: family foster or institutional care of these four probably was not responsible for their low IQs, and their mental deficiencies may even have been a determining factor in their placement.

Heston et al. [1966], comparing adults who had spent at least three months (mean = at least 24.7 months) in a foundling home during their childhood with adults who had not had this experience, found no difference between the mean IQ scores of the two groups (99.3 and 98.4).

The remainder of the studies that provide IQ scores for subjects while in care or at discharge consistently show below-average scores. The New York City subjects of Festinger's

[1983] research had an mean IQ of 93.6 while in care, while Zimmerman's [1982] sample had a mean IQ of 84. The mean IQ scores of the children in the Fanshel and Shinn study [1978] at Time I (near the time of admission into care) were as follows: mean full-scale IQ for infants (ages zero to two), 91.71; for toddlers (two to five years), mean full-scale IQ was 88.61; and for school-aged children (six and older), mean full-scale IQ was 92.04. The authors noted that only the toddlers' score was below that of the standardized population.

The youths in the 1980 Fox and Arcuri study (ages four years, 11 months to 18 years, one month) had a mean IQ of 90.18. Their mean scores on the Wide Range Achievement Test (WRAT) were 95.51 on reading and 88.50 on arithmetic; the difference between the scores on the two tests was significant ($t = 5.20$, $p < .005$). In addition, each achievement test mean was significantly different from the IQ mean.

Several authors also reported that some of their participants had been diagnosed as having a learning problem of some kind. In Festinger's study, 32% of the males and 20% of the females discharged from family foster homes had moderate to severe learning problems, as did 28% of the males and 6% of the females discharged from group settings. Zimmerman stated that 5% of her sample had attended only special education classes in school.

In the 1978 Fanshel and Shinn investigation, a majority of the children were identified by their teachers as having at least one learning problem that had a major influence on their school performance: 66% at Time I, 73% at Time II, and 76% at Time III. The types of problems included intellectual capacity problems (about one quarter of the subjects); difficulty with comprehension (about one third); little motivation to learn (at least 30%); major problems with anxiety or acting out (32%); inability to follow class routines and excessive demands for attention (25%); and poor work-study habits (34% to 43% [at various times]).

Employment and Economic Stability

Fourteen of the studies reviewed reported outcome measures of employment or financial self-sufficiency, or both. Most of these studies do not provide employment rates for that portion of the general population that is comparable to the subjects formerly in care, however, so interpretation is difficult.

Triseliotis [1980] and Triseliotis and Russell [1984] provide the only direct comparisons. Triseliotis found that 80% of his Scottish subjects formerly in family foster care had a steady work record, but many of the jobs held by them were of a precarious nature: most held unskilled or semiskilled positions that were similar to those of their parents and there had been little upward mobility. Triseliotis and Russell found that about 70% of the adoptees and 50% of the institutionalized care group were regularly employed. Thus, it would appear that the family foster care and adoptive groups do relatively well, compared to those in institutions.

Within the year prior to the study, 28% of those receiving care in an institution in the Triseliotis and Russell sample had received public assistance, compared with 4% of the adoptees and 18% of Triseliotis's family foster care group; four of the eleven institutional-care respondents who benefited from public assistance had done so for over a year. About one-third of the married subjects formerly in institutional-care received such assistance versus only 2% of all British married couples with children in 1977; 28% of single subjects who had received care in institutions received public assistance, compared to 6% of all British singles. With regard to receiving public assistance then, both out-of-home care groups perform poorly relative to the group of adoptees.

Two of the studies—Festinger's [1983] study of subjects formerly in out-of-home care in New York City, and Cook et al.'s [1991] evaluation of independent living programs—provide the most extensive employment and public assistance comparisons from other data sources. Excluding disabled respondents and those in school, Festinger reported that unemployment rates were about 25% among males and 19% among females (when homemakers are counted among the employed). Without presenting comparison data, Festinger asserted that the minority females and Caucasian males in her sample experienced levels of unemployment comparable to their counterparts in the general populace, but that African American males and Caucasian females experienced proportionally higher rates of unemployment. Other data show, however, the unemployment rate for New York males over 16 years old in 1983 was only 8.9% and that for women was 8.1% [*Statistical Abstract of the United States* 1985, Table 657 (hereafter *SAUS*)]. Thus, it appears that the subjects in Festinger's sample experienced higher rates of unemployment than comparable samples in New York State at that time.

In addition, 21% of Festinger's subjects were receiving public assistance at the time of the study; an additional 21% had received it in the past but were not current recipients. The average time members of this latter group received assistance was 13 months, often starting just after their discharge from care. Those receiving assistance at the time of the study had been receiving it for about three years on average. Most were unemployed or homemakers. Ten of the 57 had part-time employment, two were disabled, and five were full-time students.

Festinger claimed that though a higher proportion of her subjects received public aid than their counterparts in the general populace, the differences were not significant. This claim is difficult to evaluate, however, for Festinger does not report the data she used for the comparison. In 1983 in New York State, 8.1% of the general populace received public aid in the form of AFDC or SSI [*SAUS* 1985: Table 640], far less than the 21% of Festinger's sample. The magnitude of this difference suggests that it is in fact significant.

Cook et al. [1991] found that 40% of their subjects who had been in care were a "cost to the community" at the time of the interview (on welfare, in jail, or on Medicaid). Thirty percent were receiving welfare compared with 5% of all youths in the general population and 24% of all youths below the National poverty level. Only 49% were employed compared to 60% of youths in the general population. The median weekly salary of youths discharged from out-of-home care was less than 80% that of the general population.

The remainder of the studies reporting findings on economic well-being are descriptive and provide in-depth information about the functioning of those formerly in out-of-home care. To interpret these studies, we will compare their data with relevant economic data from the U.S. Bureau of the Census.

Barth [1990] reported that 75% of respondents in his study were employed, with most working full-time. This rate of labor force participation approximates that of all men over age 16 in California in 1989 (78%) [SAUS 1991: Table 636], but it is far higher than the labor force participation rate for women at that time (58%). In addition, Barth reported that most of the subjects' jobs were low paying and without benefits.

Jones and Moses [1984] reported that about 33% of their subjects were unemployed, with more men than women working full time. Twenty eight percent of Jones and Moses' respondents had held no jobs since leaving high school. This unemployment rate exceeds that of the West Virginia adult population in 1983, which was 21% for men and 13% for women [SAUS 1985: Table 657].

Seventeen (85%) of Maas's [1963] subjects were gainfully employed. Two others were married females with good employment histories, and one was a university student. Only "four or five subjects, at most," had unstable job histories. Most of the respondents considered work to be important and a source of satisfaction. Eighty-one percent of the 43 ratings on involvement and feelings of adequacy at work were "normal and above."

Allerhand et al. [1966] reported that 26 of 50 former subjects (52%) in residential group homes had some means of self-support, and 22 more had attempted on their own to find jobs. In another residential group study, Frost and Jurich [1983] found that 54% of those former residents of the Villages group homes in Kansas who were at least 18 years old at follow-up were employed. This percentage rose to 64% when only those 25 or older were counted. This labor force of 25 or older participation rate fell below that of men in Kansas in 1983 (79%), but exceeded the rate for women (55%) [SAUS 1985: Table 657]. Thus, it is comparable to that of the general populace. Harari [1980] reported that 50% of her subjects were employed, a labor force participation rate below that of young men (aged 20 to 24) in California in 1980 (68%), and below that of women (63%) [U.S. Bureau of the Census, 1983, Table 67]. Twenty-eight percent of those subjects who were employed also were enrolled in some form of school. These adults worked chiefly as salespersons, clerks, secretaries, and skilled laborers.

Ferguson [1966] reported that 7% of the total sample—8% of the men and 6% of the women (when homemaking is counted as employment)—were unemployed at the age of 20; 2% of the females had never held jobs.

Fifty-nine percent of the men in Zimmerman's [1982] New Orleans sample of children formerly in out-of-home care were employed, less than the 76% labor force participation rate for Louisiana men in 1981 [SAUS 1982–1983: Table 628]. Forty-eight percent of the women were employed, the same as the 48% participation rate for adult women in Louisiana in 1981. Among the men in Zimmerman's sample, three were disabled, four were in school or in job training, five were in prison, and only one was considered "able-bodied unemployed." Among the women, six were housewives with working husbands, two were disabled, one was in prison, and five were receiving AFDC.

Meier [1965], Zimmerman [1982], and Jones and Moses [1984] cited findings regarding the "self-sufficiency" of young adults who had been in foster care. Sixty-one of the 66 adults formerly in care (92.4%) who provided complete information to Meier either were self-supporting or living within self-supporting family units. Zimmerman's subjects did not do as well; only 64% of her respondents were supported through their own or their spouse's employment. Jones and Moses found that 43% of their subjects earned their own money and another 17% had working spouses or partners; in addition, 22% received at least part of their income from their biological parents, 18% from foster parents, and 10% from other relatives.

With regard to receipt of public assistance, Zimmerman reported that 26% of her respondents were receiving public support of some kind (SSI, AFDC, prison). This is very high compared to the general adult population in Louisiana, of whom only 7.3% received public aid in the form of AFDC or SSI in 1982 [SAUS 1984: Table 653]. Zimmerman also found that 31% of her respondents were living below the poverty level, including seven who were employed. Again, this rate exceeds that of the general populace in Louisiana, where only 19% lived below the poverty level in 1982 [SAUS 1982: Table 778]. Harari found that 47% of her subjects received financial assistance, far more than the 9% of the 1980 California populace that received public aid in the form of SSI or AFDC [SAUS 1980: Table 561].

Sixteen percent of the Jones and Moses [1984] sample from West Virginia received public assistance at the time of the study, with 50% having received it at some time. This 16% rate is more than double the 7% of the West Virginia general population who received public aid (either SSI or AFDC) in 1984 [SAUS 1986: Table 645]. In addition, 25% of the Jones and Moses sample received food stamps, and 38% of them, mostly women, had used food stamps at some time. This rate compares to the 19% of the general West Virginia populace who received food stamps in 1984 [SAUS 1986: Tables 29 and 203]. SSI payments were received by 10% of the respondents.

Job satisfaction and the degree to which former recipients of out-of-home care felt that their income, regardless of source, was adequate, were reported by Triseliotis and Russell [1984], Festinger [1983], and Jones and Moses [1984]. Triseliotis and Russell stated that 40% of their adoptees and twice that proportion of the institutional-care group expressed a great or fair amount of satisfaction with their current job. Over 75% of both groups felt that their take-home pay was at least adequate, and 70% of all the subjects felt that their standard of living was fairly satisfactory or better.

Festinger's subjects were, on average, moderately satisfied with the work they were doing. Although they stated that they were satisfied with their financial situations and with the amount of money they had to spend for basic things, 53% of them felt that their incomes were below or far below that of the average American.

Seventy percent of the Jones and Moses respondents who were working indicated that they were satisfied with their current job (most of the jobs were skilled or unskilled labor), even though many of them expressed a desire to advance themselves.

One further finding regarding employment is worth noting. Festinger found that, on the whole, those who had been in care did not feel prepared for employment when they left care.

Residential Status and Housing

Residential and Housing Outcomes Achieved

Twelve of the care outcome studies include housing or residential status as a measure in their analyses. In this group are three of the better-designed studies, Quinton et al. [1986], Wolkind [1977a, 1977b], and Triseliotis and Russell [1984], all of which include direct comparison groups.

Quinton et al. reported that the British females in their study who had been children's home residents were living at the time of follow-up in worse social circumstances than a never-in-care comparison group. Forty-four percent of the former group and 24% of the latter group were living in intermediate or poor circumstances with respect to their housing and amenities.

Wolkind's study of British primiparous (pregnant for the first time) women found that those who acknowledged being separated from their parents in childhood were more likely to have housing difficulties during their first pregnancies ($\chi^2 = 7.11$, 1 df, $p < .01$), regardless of the reason why they were placed. This report did not differentiate out-of-home care placements from other forms of separation. Wolkind did, however, study the subsample of women who had been in care for at least one month. This subsample was more likely than women who had not been in care to have current poor housing conditions (44% v. 26%, $\chi^2 = 4.79$, 1 df, $p < .05$).

Triseliotis and Russell [1984] reported on the proportion of their subjects who lived with family members. One-third of the adoptees lived with their adopted parents, including two subjects who were married, and 5% lived with siblings. Only 3% of the group who had been placed in institutions were living with their biological parents, but 21% were living with biological siblings or other relatives; many felt that they had nowhere else to go.

Cook et al.'s [1991] comparison of outcomes for children discharged from care and those for the general population found that 39% of the subjects formerly in care were living with extended family compared to 53% of youths in the general population. Living with extended family was the most frequent arrangement at both the time of discharge and at the interview. Twelve percent reported that they had sought housing assistance since leaving care and 10% had used public shelters. Approximately 25% had spent at least one night without a place to live. Thirty-two percent had experienced five or more different living arrangements since discharge, and the majority (57%) were not satisfied with their current living arrangement and indicated they would like to move.

Festinger [1983] does not provide comparative data with regard to the quality of housing but does regarding mobility. She reports that compared to other New Yorkers their age, more respondents who had been in care who were living in New York City, regardless of ethnicity or type of placement, had moved at least once. Barth's [1990] sample experienced severe housing problems, with 29% of his subjects reporting that there was a time that they had no home or were moving every week or more frequently.

The studies described above all suggest that finding stable housing is particularly difficult for those who were once in care. On the other hand, Zimmerman [1982] reported that the housing pattern of the children in her study was roughly typical of that for New Orleans as a whole. Sixty-eight percent of her respondents lived independently: 49% lived in private rental housing, 12% lived in public housing, and 7% lived in homes they owned. Eighteen percent lived with relatives and 10% were in a correctional facility; the situations of the remaining 5% were unknown. She also noted that all of the single-parent heads of households were female (34% of the women).

The remaining studies provide descriptive information about housing but lack comparative data; however, they can be compared to relevant state-level housing data. Jones and Moses [1984] reported a low proportion of children who were formerly in care living independently. Only 35% of their respondents were heads of their own households, 5% were in jail, and 3% resided in residential or group care. This compares unfavorably to an adult imprisonment rate of 1% in West Virginia in 1983 [SAUS 1986: Table 322], and a .3% admission rate into psychiatric hospitals in the United States in 1983 [SAUS 1986: Table 170].

Meier's [1965] study, while dated, involved some of the oldest subjects; thereby providing a better assessment of potential long-term problems. She found that all of the women in her Minnesota study were the "mistresses of their own home," either as wives or as heads of households. Sixty percent of the men were married and living with their spouse, less than the 81% of American men in 1966 who were married and living with their spouse [*SAUS* 1967: Table 33]. One additional man in her study (3%) lived with his wife in the home of her parents. Twenty-three percent of the men were single and lived on their own, exceeding the 17% single rate among American men aged 25 to 29 in 1966 [*SAUS* 1967: Table 33]. Two men (7%) lived with their former foster parents, one man was in jail, and one man was in the armed services. Meier added that 57% of the respondents were buying or already owned their own homes, a sign of stability. This stability was not shared by all of the subjects, however, for some of them reported having changed residences frequently since discharge; one had moved "about 200" times.

The subjects of Allerhand et al.'s study [1966] were younger than those of Meier (average of 18 v. 30 years), which may account for some of their differences. Seventy percent of these young men lived in their own homes or in some other independent situation. Twelve percent remained in family foster care or group homes, and 8% lived in some sort of institution. Eight percent were enrolled in schools or colleges away from home, and one respondent (2%) was in the armed services.

The three Scottish studies seem to reveal less independent living than the American ones. Ferguson [1966], for example, reported when subjects were 20 years old (two years after discharge), 27% of the males were in the armed forces or merchant marine. Thirty percent of all respondents were living with their foster parents, 3% (all female) were living with their biological parents, and an additional 11% were living with other relatives. Eighteen percent of the women were living with their husbands, 11% of the sample had housing provided with their jobs, and 28% of the men and 16% of the women lived on their own.

Although Triseliotis [1980] does not provide details, he does state that 35% of his Scottish young people were living with their foster parents, while 25% were on their own. An additional 25% had "precarious" living arrangements: they moved frequently, some had unsuccessfully attempted to live with their biological families, and they generally felt "rootless and drifting."

Thirty of Harari's [1980] 34 California subjects left the homes of their foster parents when they exited from care, usually upon reaching the age of 18 or becoming emancipated minors. For 27% of these, their first living arrangement was a shared apartment with a roommate; 27% moved in with a boyfriend or husband, 13% moved in with relatives, and 3% moved in with friends; 7% rented their own apartments, and 23% made some other type of arrangement. Sixty-three percent rated their first living arrangement as very good, 13% as somewhat good, 7% as neutral, 7% as somewhat bad, and 10% as very bad. During the first five years after leaving care, they moved an average of 3.9 times, leading the author to term them "not extremely mobile" [Harari 1980: 148].

Triseliotis and Russell [1984] found relatively high satisfaction with current housing among their subjects: 80% of the adoptees and 70% of the sample from institutions expressed this sentiment. Five percent of the former group and 12% of the latter stated that they were dissatisfied with their housing. Festinger reported that, on the whole, her respondents felt more positive than negative about their homes and neighborhoods, but that the level of satisfaction generally was moderate; those living in houses seemed to be more pleased than others.

The residences of those subjects in the Jones and Moses [1984] investigation who were interviewed in their own homes were assessed by the interviewers. Space, structure, furnishings, and housekeeping were evaluated. "Adequate" ratings were achieved by 70% to 78% of the households; only 5% to 7% received "inadequate" scores.

Although Festinger [1983] found that nearly all of her respondents (98%) had been discharged into their own care, they had not felt well prepared to undertake this responsibility. One-quarter of them stated that they had received "a lot" of preparation, 23% "some," 9% "a little," and 43% "very little" or "not at all." Harari reported that her subjects felt they had availed themselves of help from social services with housing significantly less often than they needed to ($p < .05$).

Homelessness among Former Foster Children

In the past eight years, several studies of homeless persons have revealed that a disproportionate number of them have spent some time in out-of-home care during their childhoods. Six of these studies are described in part, the focus being on those findings that pertain to out-of-home care. Appendix C provides a summary of relevant information regarding these studies. These six studies supplement the 29 core studies discussed in this book.

The first study of homeless adults to report findings regarding childhood placement in out-of-home care was conducted by Crystal [1984] in New York City, in 1982 and 1983. Intake assessments were completed on 8,051 men and women (22% of the sample were women) applying for emergency shelter during that period. Crystal reports that 7% of the women and 3% of the men primarily grew up in out-of-home care or institutions. Many more reported that they had been in a family foster home or institution for some part of their childhood.

In the spring and summer of 1985, Susser et al. [1987] interviewed 223 male, first-time users of New York City shelters, as well as a representative sample of 695 men already residing in those shelters. The authors found that 23% of the first-time shelter users had been placed in family foster care, group homes, and/or other special residences before the age of 17. In the broader sample of current shelter residents, the authors found that 17% had been placed in similar out-of-home care settings before age 17.

Sosin et al. [1990] conducted a two-wave longitudinal study of homeless adults in Minneapolis beginning in November 1985 and ending in May 1986. They interviewed 338 homeless adults (85% male) in a cross-sectional sample and 113 homeless adults (77% male) who were designated as recent arrivals to homelessness (current homeless spell less than 14 days in length). They reported that 39% of the cross-section had been placed in a family foster home, group home, or institution at some time before their 18th birthday. Thirty-five percent of the recent-arrivals sample had experienced at least one of those types of placement.

In a comparative study of 181 homeless persons (63% male) and 355 (74% male) poor, domiciled persons in Chicago free-meal programs in 1986, Sosin et al. [1988] reported that 15% of adults in their sample who were ever homeless and 7% of adults who had never been homeless had experienced out-of-home care (family foster home, group home, institution) prior to their 18th birthday.

Using data collected from 74 homeless persons (90% male) in Lexington, Kentucky, during the winter and spring of 1988, Mangine et al. [1990] determined that 16% had been "in foster care (a ward of the state) as a child (birth to 18 years old)." They reported that this rate was four times the rate for the local, general, adult population, as estimated by Royse and Wiehe [1989].

Susser et al. [1991] compared three samples of homeless psychiatric patients ($N = 512$) to a sample of never-homeless psychiatric patients ($N = 271$) in New York City and found the rate of childhood placement to be substantially higher for the homeless group. Fifteen percent of the homeless group had experienced family foster care and 10% had experienced group home placement. By comparison, among the never-homeless sample, 2% had experienced family foster care and

1% had experienced group home placement. (Unfortunately, these authors did not report the combined proportion of individuals who had experienced family foster care *or* group home care.)

Using only the state psychiatric hospital samples from the above study, Susser et al. [1991] compared those individuals who had been in out-of-home care with those who had not, relative to the experience of adult homelessness. They found that 79% of those patients who had been in family foster care experienced homelessness as an adult, compared to 25% of those who had not been in family foster care. Eighty percent of those who had been in group homes were later homeless, compared to 25% of those who had not been in group homes. In logistic regressions predicting homelessness among these state hospital patients, a history of family foster care or group home placement significantly predicted adult homelessness, even after controlling for age, ethnicity, gender, psychiatric diagnosis, and substance abuse history. Susser et al. suggested, however, that although childhood placement strongly predicts homelessness, it may not be a *cause* of homelessness. Placement may be a result of other childhood experiences, such as the death of a parent, poverty, or abuse or neglect, which may themselves be causally related to homelessness. Consequently, placement would function only as a proxy for these other causes of homelessness.

Adult Self-Sufficiency: An Outcomes Summary and Predictors

Education

The studies reported above are fairly unanimous in their findings that the level of educational attainment of persons who had been in care is below the average attainment of those citizens of comparable age in the same state or country. Excluding the Rest and Watson [1984] study, which had only

13 subjects, the reported findings indicate that between 15% and 56% of the subjects formerly in care had not completed high school—a minimal requirement for those hoping to achieve adult self-sufficiency. While in school, members of this group functioned at a level that was below average and below their capacity. As might be expected, they were more likely to pursue vocational or job training than to attend college.

These findings cannot be interpreted to mean that low educational achievement is a result of experiencing out-of-home care. None of the studies were designed to answer this question. The Casey Family Project, however, found that one-third of the subjects were behind grade level when placed and the same proportion were behind grade level at discharge [Fanshel et al. 1990]. These findings and those reported by other researchers clearly indicate that out-of-home care, while not necessarily detrimental, does not successfully compensate for early deficiencies in the lives of children.

In reviewing these findings and those in the following sections and chapters, one should keep in mind that successes do occur. Eight percent to 39% of the subjects (excluding Rest and Watson's study) in the reviewed studies had attended college. Nevertheless, the relatively poor academic performance of children in care, which has been confirmed by research such as that presented above, should be a concern for professionals and lay persons working with this population of children and for legislators and other policymakers. Education has been demonstrated to be associated with such important features of life as adult employment, well-being, and interpersonal involvement. Those who were formerly in care have rated it as one of the three most important areas for agencies to stress in discharge planning [Festinger 1983], and improvements in education are being explored as part of the child welfare reform movement.

Our search for predictors of positive outcomes can inform

this effort to bring about change. Findings regarding type of placement are mixed. Festinger [1983] found that youth discharged from family foster care completed more schooling than those from group care settings. Triseliotis and Russell [1984], however, found both adoptees and subjects receiving institutional care to have completed more schooling than children in family foster care. Higher socioeconomic status of foster parents, better parenting on the part of foster parents, and a permissive foster home were all found to be associated with academic progress and increases in nonverbal IQ scores [Fanshel and Shinn 1978; Palmer 1976]. In addition, the educational aspirations and expectations of foster children were similar to those of foster parents [Triseliotis 1980].

Factors leading to placement were found to be associated with educational outcomes in several studies. Children who were physically abused before entering care achieved lower educational levels, whereas those placed because of the death of a parent achieved higher levels [Fanshel et al. 1990; Palmer 1976]. The younger the child at placement, the fewer years of schooling he or she attained [Fanshel & Shinn 1978].

With respect to within-placement factors, there was moderate support for the expected negative effects of multiple placements on educational achievement [Zimmerman 1982; Palmer 1976; Festinger 1983; Cook et al. 1991], and no relationship was found between education and time in care [Fanshel & Shinn 1978; Fox & Arcuri 1980; Zimmerman 1982; Cook et al. 1991] or discharge disposition [Fanshel & Shinn 1978; Zimmerman 1982]. On the other hand, children who had only one long-term caseworker were more likely to make good academic progress [Palmer 1976]. No relationship between the amount of contact with the biological family during placement and educational achievement was found; however, the child's identifying with the foster family *was* a predictor of good academic performance [Festinger 1983; Palmer 1976].

Employment

To sum up, with regard to employment and economic stability, the majority of the studies reviewed here indicate that a majority (64% to 92%) of former foster children are self-supporting adults. One of the more recent and larger studies [Cook et al. 1991], however, found that slightly less than half of older foster youths (≥ 16 at discharge) were employed at the time of the follow-up interview (2.5 to four years after discharge). It also seems that for many, perhaps even most, employment is steady but precarious. Unemployment rate estimates range from 25% to 41% for males and around 20% for females. One study estimates that as many as 28% of those formerly in care have never held a job. Although results across studies vary widely (from 4% to 47%), it seems that approximately 25% of those formerly in care receive public assistance as adults.

Families, both biological and foster, appear to provide financial support for a significant proportion of adults who were in care as children. Comparison data are not available, but this situation does not appear to be greatly different from what one would expect to find for young adults in the general population.

Those discharged from family foster homes do better economically than those who resided in group settings, and adoptees do better than those who were in care [Festinger 1983; Triseliotis & Russell 1984]. There is some evidence that identification with the foster family is associated with improved economic outcomes [Palmer 1976], whereas closeness and contact with the biological family were not associated with improved economic outcomes [Festinger 1983; Triseliotis & Russell 1984]. Finishing high school before discharge from out-of-home care and having at least one job while in out-of-home care were positively related to maintaining a job for at least one year. On the other hand, being black, non-Hispanic; emotionally disturbed or handicapped; and having drug problems and chronic health problems were all negatively associated with maintaining a job [Cook et al. 1991].

Conflicting findings exist with regard to number of placements, and no association was found in any study between economic outcomes and either age at placement or caseworker activity. However, Cook et al.'s evaluation of independent living programs did find that those youth who received an increasing number of skills training in five "core skill areas" (money, consumer, credit, education, and employment) were more likely to maintain a job for at least one year.

Housing

The majority of the studies reported here indicate that most (roughly 60% to 70%) of the subjects were living independently in adequate housing. Jones and Moses [1984] diverge widely from this finding, reporting that only 35% of their subjects were living independently. The three Scottish studies generally reported lower levels as well. Sizable numbers of subjects were found to be still living with their foster parents or friends and relatives. Biological families appear to be a source of minimal housing support.

This limited body of research suggested few predictors of poor housing outcomes. Those subjects who were adopted or resided in family foster homes appear to achieve more positive outcomes than those in group or institutional settings [Festinger 1983; Triseliotis & Russell 1984].

All of the studies of homeless persons cited in this book reveal significantly high rates of childhood out-of-home placement for homeless adults, ranging from 17% to 39%. They leave unexplained, however, the process by which childhood placement and adult homelessness are linked. Piliavin et al. [1987: 27–28] offer several explanations.

> It may be that many young people put in foster homes and institutions have severe emotional or behavioral problems which, if not abated by these experiences,

make them vulnerable to various adult problems and crises, including long-term homelessness. Alternatively, out-of-home care may itself be debilitating, leaving its recipients relatively less able to manage independently and conventionally as adults. Finally, young people who receive out-of-home care may have weak family ties, generated in part by the conditions necessitating care and augmented perhaps by the experience of foster care. As adults, these individuals would be likely to lack family support networks that could provide them major resources at times of economic crises. In such circumstances these individuals would be vulnerable to homelessness.

Others have more explicitly faulted the out-of-home care system for failing to adequately prepare youths leaving out-of-home care for independent living. Demchak [1985] cites a New York State Supreme Court decision pertaining to youths formerly in care. The court found that the state and city social service officials had failed to discharge their duties under state law to supervise youths in care until the age of 21 and to prepare them to live independently. In addition, it found that these young people had suffered irreparable injury because of their homelessness, including the potential for denial of public assistance because they lacked permanent addresses. Demchak notes that in New York City each year, over 1,700 children in care reach the age of 18 and are discharged from placements to independent living. She reports that New York City's Coalition for the Homeless found that 7,500 young people in the city who had aged out of care were living in public shelters, transit terminals, subways, and on the streets. Understanding the link between out-of-home care and homelessness is clearly an urgent task.

Chapter 6

Behavioral Adjustment

Adult functioning can be judged not only by the attainment of self-sufficiency, but also by the avoidance of self-destructive or unlawful acts. This chapter focuses on the limited number of studies that have looked at behavioral maladjustment as evidenced by criminal behavior and chemical dependency among persons who were in care as children.

Criminal Behavior

Eleven of the 29 studies reviewed provided information on criminal activity. Quinton et al.'s [1986] study had the strongest overall methodological approach. Findings from this study may not readily generalize, however, since it had a relatively small sample and was restricted to British women; the small sample creates further limitations, given the study's analysis of phenomena that occur infrequently, particularly for women.

Among the British women investigated by Quinton et al., those who had been in care were more likely than the control group members to have a criminal record. According to the self-reports, 22% of the former group and none of the latter had such records (χ^2 = 8.59, p < .02). This rate of convictions for women who had been in care is higher than that of other reports.

Two other studies judged to be of moderate quality reported on criminal behavior. One [Triseliotis & Russell 1984] included a comparison group but also had a relatively small sample (N = 159) and involved subjects in Scotland. The second, by Festinger [1983], had a larger sample but significant dropout problems. Although Festinger does not include a specific comparison group, she does provide comparative rates for the U.S. general population and the New York City population. The relatively young age of the subjects of both of these studies and that in the study by Quinton et al. is less of a problem in this analysis than it was in examining adult self-sufficiency, since criminal behavior tends to decline with age. Group differences therefore are relatively more likely to manifest themselves at earlier ages, if they exist at all.

In two Scottish studies, Triseliotis [1980] and Triseliotis and Russell [1984] reported court appearances of their subjects rather than arrests. Triseliotis and Russell found that 9% of the adoptees and 8% of the group receiving institutional care had juvenile hearings; there are no significant differences between these rates and those found by Triseliotis in the earlier study. More subjects in the later study, however, had appeared in adult court: 27% of adoptees and 40% of those in residential care versus 13% of the family foster care group. Overall, 32% of the adoptees and 43% of the institutional care group had appeared in juvenile or adult proceedings. Neither study provides rates by sex of the subject.

Festinger [1983] reported arrest and conviction rates obtained from the New York State Division of Criminal Justice Services, which lists adult offenses committed in that state. She found that, since discharge from care, 33% of her male subjects and 5% of the female subjects had been arrested for either a misdemeanor or felony. All but one of the females had been arrested only once, while this was true for only half of the males. Sixty-eight percent of the males who had been arrested had been charged with at least one felony. After controlling for age and ethnicity, Festinger concluded that "the proportion of graduates from foster care who had been arrested was almost identical to the proportion of males with records of arrest in the general population."

Although there were problems with missing data regarding convictions, it appeared that about 38% of both males and females in the sample who were arrested were later convicted. The number of study subjects who were convicted was too small to permit comparisons with estimates from the general population.

Ferguson's [1966] study is one of the better-designed ones with respect to sample size and attrition. The date and setting (Scotland), however, may reduce its relevance to current practices in the United States. While Ferguson's study primarily focuses on adolescents in care, it does provide comparative reference data to better judge the significance of the outcomes. Ferguson found that, of the Scottish subjects who had been in care, 1% of the females and 6% of the males had been convicted of at least one crime while still in school (aged 15 years or younger). This rate for males was higher than that reported for the general population of males in Glasgow. The rate of convictions increased between the ages of 16 and 18 to 4% of the females and almost 23% of the males. The conviction rate for a sample of Glasgow males who had left school at age 14, by comparison, was only 12%.

The conviction rate of those in the Ferguson sample declines between ages 18 and 20, to 3% of the females and 15% of the males. All told, by the time the respondents reached the age of 20, 7% of the females and 31% of the males had been convicted of at least one offense; over half of these crimes had been committed between the ages of 15 and 17.

The next cluster of studies addressing this outcome [Zimmerman 1982; Jones & Moses 1984; Barth 1990; Frost & Jurich 1983] do not include explicit comparison groups or reference data. As such, these studies are difficult to interpret, especially since age-specific data on arrest histories are scarce.

Arrest histories for those age 18 and older over the whole life course are available, however, for comparison purposes. Zimmerman reported that 28% of the males in her sample in New Orleans and 6% of the females had been convicted of crimes and served at least six months in prison; about half of these were in jail at the time of the study. National data suggest that between 20% and 25% of all men are arrested by age 18, and that 50% to 60% are arrested at some point in their lifetime. For women the rates are about one-fourth those of men [Blumstein et al. 1986]. In addition, in 1981 only about 2% of the general adult populace of Louisiana was imprisoned [SAUS 1984: Table 320]. Thus, Zimmerman's subjects experienced high levels of arrest and imprisonment. An additional 15% of Zimmerman's subjects had spent a few hours or overnight in jail for minor offenses.

Zimmerman created another variable that reflected, in part, criminal behavior. She categorized her subjects by their individual functioning levels, which included measures of adherence to the law, self-support, and taking care of their own children. She determined that 33% were functioning inadequately in one or more of these basic areas of societal expectation.

Forty-seven percent of those studied by Jones and Moses [1984] had been picked up or arrested by the police. Jones and Moses found that 11% of their sample had been arrested once and 26% more than once, while 10% were picked up but not arrested. Over half of those arrested were convicted, and over half of these went to jail; in all, 22% of the sample had spent time in jail.

Barth [1990] found slightly lower rates of involvement in illegal activity. Almost one-third (31%) of his sample of young adults had been arrested, and 26% had spent time in jail or prison. Compared to national data, these rates are normal.

Frost and Jurich [1983] reported that of their subjects who were 18 or older, 9% had been arrested for felonies and 16% had been arrested for misdemeanors. All of the felony arrests involved males, as did nine of the 12 misdemeanor arrests. Thus, 26% of the males had been arrested for felonies and 33% had been arrested for misdemeanors. This is high relative to national levels, for data compiled by Blumstein et al. [1986] suggest that around 15% of males are arrested for F.B.I. index offenses at least once during their lifetime. Overall, 15% of Frost and Urich's subjects (male and female) had spent time in jail or prison, while 26% of the males (11 of the 43) had spent time in jail or prison.

The remaining two studies that attempted to address criminal behavior as an outcome [Meier 1965; Allerhand et al. 1966] are dated, provide no basis for comparison, and contain samples that are too small for the drawing of conclusions.

In summary, as with the general population, male subjects who were in out-of-home care engage in criminal behavior to a greater extent than do females. Furthermore, with the exception of Festinger's study, the available data suggest that this group of males engages in criminal behavior as young adults more often than do young males in the general population or those placed in adoptive homes. Arrest rates reported in these studies vary from about 25% to over 40%, and rates of court appearances for children formerly in care were about 13% to 20%. Over half of those arrested are commonly convicted, while 14% to 22% of subjects were reported to have spent time in jail. Not all studies used the same measures, so few studies are included in each of the ranges reported here.

Chemical Dependency

Alcohol Use

Five studies examined alcohol use: Robins [1966], Triseliotis and Russell [1984], Festinger [1983], Barth [1990] and Cook et al. [1991]. In one of the best designed of the 29 studies reviewed, Robins compared male subjects who had been given a diagnosis of alcoholism with those considered "well" (in that they had no clinical diagnosis). The alcoholics reported a higher rate of having lived away from both parents than did those with no disease (76% v. 39%, $p < .05$). Not all of those who had lived apart from their parents had been placed in care; some subjects may have been hospitalized or lived with relatives for extended periods.

The percentage of subjects who drank alcoholic beverages was reported in two of the moderately well-designed studies. Triseliotis and Russell [1984] compared subjects age 20 and 21 cared for in institutions with a sample of adoptees. Ninety percent of the former group and 81% of the latter drank. Triseliotis and Russell also compared their participants to the general population. They reported that their subjects had fewer alcohol-related problems than did the general Scottish population, but felt that this may be explained, at least in part, by the relatively young age of their subjects and the tendency for drinking problems to increase with age. Cook et al. [1991], however, also reported lower alcohol consumption in their U.S. study, even when those formerly in care, (age 18 to 23) were compared to a similar age cohort in the general population. Forty-two percent of the discharged out-of-home care population reported alcohol use over the previous 30-day period, compared to 62% of the general population age 18 to 24 years.

Festinger [1983] provided several details about the history of alcohol consumption of her subjects. Over 41% of the males and 28% of the females began drinking before the age of 16. Twenty-nine percent of the males and 12% of the females drank at least three times per week, and 62% of the males and 36% of the females had drunk enough during the month preceding the study to "feel high." A comparison with a group of children discharged from care five years earlier, found no significant differences in the age at which they began drinking or the amount they drank, suggesting some stability in these findings. There also was no difference between the subjects who had been in care and the respondents in a general population study in the proportion who drank alcoholic beverages; however, it was found that African Americans in the out-of-home care group drank more frequently to handle tension and drank "too much" more often than did African Americans in the general population.

One additional study is noteworthy. Barth found that the proportion of youth who reported drinking once a week or more (19%) was comparable to a random sample of high school students.

Conclusions are difficult to draw in this area. The Robins study offers the strongest evidence of increased risk of alcohol-related problems for subjects who were once in care. Festinger offers limited support for this position but only for the subpopulation of African Americans, while Barth's findings suggest that drinking is not a particular problem for youths in care. Overall, the available information does not support any firm conclusions.

Drug Use

Barth [1990] found that, unlike the data on drinking, the proportion of subjects reporting use of street drugs while in out-of-home care (56%) compared unfavorably to use by the general population of high school students. (Barth did not provide comparable figures for high school students.) In addition, this usage rate had not declined since leaving out-of-home care. Cook et al. [1991], however, in a study larger and more representative than Barth's, found rates of marijuana and other illegal drug use for youths discharged from care to be almost identical to those reported for the general population age 18 to 24.

Festinger [1983] reported that 81% of the males and 66% of the females in her study had used drugs of some sort in the year preceding the study, usually marijuana and cocaine; tranquilizers were seldom used. Thirty percent of the respondents had used drugs at least once or twice a week during the previous year; almost 29% of the males and 14% of the females had used at least one drug practically every day. Forty-nine percent of the males and 65% of the females either never had used drugs or else had done so no more often than twice a month. Forty-three percent of the males and 29% of the females had begun using drugs before the age of 15. No comparisons with the general population were provided.

Festinger's sample of children in care discharged in 1975 compared unfavorably with a similar sample of children who had been discharged in 1970. More of the 1975 subjects had used drugs at least once a week during the year preceding the study (31% v. 14%); and although about the same percentage used drugs and about the same amount of drugs was used, the 1975 group began their usage at a younger age and used drugs more often than the 1970 group. These results suggest that drug use may be on the rise in the out-of-home care population.

Although Harari [1980] did not provide specific proportions of her subjects who used alcohol or drugs, she did indicate that their usage had decreased since leaving care. Festinger reported similar findings: of her subjects who had ever used drugs, 45% had decreased their usage over the years, while 37% had increased usage.

Clearly, the data regarding drug usage are even less conclusive than those regarding alcohol.

Behavior: An Outcomes Summary and Predictors

Crime

Data from the above studies indicate that arrest rates for males formerly in foster care generally fall between 25% and 35% but may be well over 40%. Of those arrested, one-quarter to one-half are subsequently convicted. Arrest rates appear much lower for females (approximately 10%). Relevant comparisons are difficult to find in the reviewed studies. While arrest and conviction rates, particularly for males, are higher than what one would expect in the general population, they may not be widely different once race and socioeconomic status are controlled for. With regard to criminal behavior, family foster care subjects fared better than those who had been in group care or lived with relatives.

Contrary to the current emphasis on family preservation, several sources of evidence indicate that increased ties with family and community of origin are associated with higher criminal behavior. Discharge from foster care to the home of a family member was associated with convictions, as was discharge to independent living [Zimmerman 1982]. Increased family visits were associated with a return home and increased criminal activity [Triseliotis & Russell 1984; Zimmerman 1982]. Boys placed in out-of-home care whose fathers lived at home had a significantly higher rate of adult deviance [McCord et al. 1960]. On the other hand, a positive adjustment in a family foster home was associated with positive adult behavior [Triseliotis 1980; Zimmerman 1982].

No consistent relationship is reported between the reason for out-of-home care placement (e.g., type of abuse or neglect) and subsequent criminal behavior [Fanshel et al. 1990; Festinger 1983; Kraus 1981]. Changes in out-of-home care placement were associated with increased criminal behavior [Ferguson 1966; Kraus 1981]; this was not seen for time in placement [Kraus 1981] or age at placement [Kraus 1981; Triseliotis & Russell 1984].

Clearly, the potential for spurious associations exists here—for example, several authors noted associations between adult criminal behavior and adjustment problems or behavioral problems while in care—and findings must be interpreted with caution.

Drug and Alcohol Abuse

There is little solid evidence that alcohol or other drug use may be a particular problem for those who were formerly in care (relative to comparison groups). Some evidence suggests increases in drug-related problems may reflect increases in the general population. The problems that do exist seem to decline as the subjects grow older. Those who lived in group settings seem to fare worse than those who were either adopted or in family foster care.

Alcohol and drug use was not found to be associated with age at placement or number of placements. On the other hand, there does appear to be a negative association between adjustment in out-of-home care and level of alcohol consumption [Triseliotis & Russell 1984].

Chapter 7

Family and Social Support

The ability to form and maintain supportive family and social relationships is an indicator of a person's general maturity, functioning, and integration in the community. In addition, forming and maintaining supportive family and social relationships may influence a person's ability to remain self-sufficient, make healthy adjustments, and achieve overall well-being as an adult. As children, individuals formerly in out-of-home care suffered abuse and neglect, separation from their parents and community, and instability in their home environment. Can they overcome these deficiencies in their adult lives? In this chapter we examine the outcomes achieved by individuals who were in out-of-home care as children in four categories of family and social support: marriage, parenting, relationship with their extended family, and social relationships.

Family Life

Marital Outcomes Achieved

Fourteen of the 29 studies included in this review report marriage, divorce, and cohabitation rates of the subjects. Six of the 14 studies provide some basis for comparing these rates to those of the general population or to a comparison group. The range in ages of the subjects reduces the possibilities for comparisons across studies.

Time since out-of-home care is critical in judging a study's utility with respect to this outcome. Not surprisingly, the studies with the youngest respondents [Ferguson 1966; Maas 1963] reported the lowest marriage rates (13% and 15%, respectively). Meier [1965], with subjects in their late twenties and thirties, reported a marriage rate of 93%. The median marriage rate for the 14 studies is 30%, and the mean is 37%. The Meier rate may be an outlier, for the next highest rate is 56%. It should also be noted that the Meier study is one of the oldest ones reviewed.

Cultural differences could also be expected to influence findings with respect to marriage. The three lowest rates were found in studies of subjects from Scotland and England [Maas 1963; Ferguson 1966; Wolkind 1977a; 1977b].

On the basis of strength of research design, six studies are of particular interest and are the focus of the following discussion: Quinton et al. [1986], Wolkind [1977a, 1977b], Triseliotis and Russell [1984], Festinger [1983], Cook et al. [1991] and Cook [1992]. All six provide some basis for comparison. The oldest was published in 1977; the others were published after 1980. All have moderate to large sample sizes. The dropout rate, however, is a serious problem for four of them (Triseliotis & Russell; Festinger; Cook et al.; and Cook).

Using the criteria described in Chapter 3 to evaluate the studies' outcomes, the strongest of these four studies is found to be that conducted by Quinton et al. This study has no major flaws, and relative to the other studies, it has an exceptionally low attrition rate (14% for the out-of-home care group).

Quinton et al. compared a group of British women, ages 21 to 27, who had spent part of their childhood in a children's home (called *ex-cares* in the study) with a control group who never had been in care. The ex-care subjects were less likely than the controls to be in a stable cohabiting situation. Of those with children (61% of ex-cares and 37% of controls), 61% of the ex-cares and 100% of the controls were living with the father of all of their children (χ^2 = 6.52, 1 df, p < .02); 22% of the ex-cares and none of the controls lacked a male partner (Fisher's exact probability test, p = .039). The ex-cares were also more likely than the controls to have had substantial difficulties in sexual or love relationships (22% v. 2%, χ^2 = 6.67, 1 df, p < .01), to have broken up with one or more partners (38% v. 7%, χ^2 = 12.7, 1 df, p < .001), and to have married men who had psychiatric disorders, were criminals or addicts, or had difficulties in relationships (51% v. 13%, χ^2 = 11.32, 1 df, p < .001).

Another British study [Wolkind 1977a; 1977b] was among the four best designs exploring marital outcomes. Compared to the Quinton et al. study, Wolkind's out-of-home care sample is smaller and the study is older. The sample consisted of primiparous women in England, divided into two groups based upon whether they had experienced a separation from one or both of their parents during childhood. Women who admitted to a separation from their parents in childhood were less likely to have married than those who had not (χ^2 = 11.48, 2 df, p < .01). These separations were of various types and durations, and were further subdivided into those occurring within a "stable" or a "disrupted" context; all subjects who had been placed in the care of the local authorities were considered to be in the disrupted group. Of those who had been separated from their parents, the ones within a stable context were more likely than the disrupted group to be married (χ^2 = 20.57, 1 df, p < .001).

The major drawback of Triseliotis and Russell's [1984] study is its high attrition rate (47%). In addition, Triseliotis did not report findings from the earlier study [1980] of out-of-home care subjects, leaving only the adoption and institutional-care subjects from the later study for comparison.

About one-half of all Triseliotis and Russell's Scottish subjects of had been married at least once (49% of those who had been adopted and 55% of those who had been placed in residential care). About 20% of those who had ever married had been separated or divorced (24% of the adoptees and 18% of those in institutional care). Of those who had been divorced, 40% had remarried. All 18 currently married adoptees reported that their marriages were stable; three had had marital problems in the past that had been cleared up. The group that had been cared for in institutions appeared to fare worse. The number of subjects, however, was quite small. Five members (28%) of this group who were married at the time of the study reported having marital problems; 32% expressed some dissatisfaction with their marriages.

The fourth study, by Festinger [1983], is from the United States. It is comparable to the Triseliotis and Russell study in that it has a high dropout rate (54%), but it lacks a direct comparison group. Festinger does, however, provide comparison data from several other surveys. Marriage rates among her 1975 New York City sample were 30% (25% of the males and 47% of the females), with 24% married at the time of the study. Festinger compared these results with those of several national general population studies and found that those who had been in out-of-home care as children were less likely to marry than others in the general population—as much as 40% less likely in some cases; this was also true for the subjects of the 1970 out-of-home care survey she used for comparative purposes. When compared to the general population in New York City, however, those who had been in out-of-home care from the 1975 group were *no* less likely to marry, with one exception: African American females who had been in care were less likely to marry than were African American females in the city's general population; this difference was smaller than the comparison with African American females in the national surveys.

In addition, 18% of Festinger's subjects were living with a partner at the time of the study; of these, there was a higher percentage of females than males. A total of 42% of the respondents were either married or living with a partner (39% of the males and 60% of the females). These marriages or partnerships had lasted, on average, for over two years.

About one-quarter of Festinger's sample had been divorced or separated. She found no difference between the rate for her sample and that in general population surveys.

Cook's [1992] study employing data from the 1988 National Survey of Families compared 107 adults who had been in care as children and 12,910 adults who had not been placed. Forty-five percent of the former group were married, compared to 53% of the latter. The former group also reported significantly lower marital happiness even when controlling for sociodemographic differences between the two groups.

In contrast to the findings above, Cook et al. [1991] found that their subjects discharged from care were no less likely to have ever married than were either youths in the general population or youths living in poverty. This study was also subject to a high attrition rate (51%).

A fairly consistent picture emerges from the above studies. Compared to the general population, or to persons who did not experience a separation from their biological family, persons who were in care as children are less likely to form stable marriages. Comparisons with more similar populations like adoptees, however, [Triseliotis & Russell 1984] show little difference. Festinger's and Cook et al.'s comparisons to the general population also revealed little difference, but the high dropout rate of these studies raises the possibility of positive bias. That is, the subjects located might be expected to have more stable lives in general and to be in more stable relationships than those who dropped out.

Two studies examining this outcome [Maas 1963; Ferguson 1966] are of little use because of the young age of the subjects.

As one might expect, these studies report the lowest marriage rates (13% and 15% respectively).

At the other end of the spectrum, the study by Meier [1965] involves the oldest subjects (age 28 to 32) and the highest reported marriage rate (93%). Compared with the general population, about the same percentage of Meier's male subjects who had been in care had been married, but a higher percentage of them had been separated from their spouses for various reasons (4% of the general population as compared to 14% of the subjects). More female subjects who had been in care as children had been married than females in the general population (100% v. 89%), and more also had been separated from their spouses (12% v. 5%); however, more of the first group were living with a spouse at the time of the study than was the case in the general population.

None of the five remaining studies that furnish data on marital outcomes [Harari 1980; Zimmerman 1982; Frost & Jurich 1983; Jones & Moses 1984; and Rest & Watson 1984] provide a direct comparison group in their design, and all have significant attrition problems. Rest and Watson had only 13 subjects on which to base a marriage rate of 54%. Zimmerman produced a similar rate (56%) with her much larger sample ($N = 170$); her attrition rate, however, is the highest of this group, at 64%, and may lead to some positive bias. The remaining three studies produce marriage rates ranging from 21% to 32%. This range is probably a reasonable estimate of the marriage rate for adults in their twenties who had been in care as children.

Two of the studies described above also included comparative data on marital satisfaction. Quinton et al. [1986] found that, of their respondents who had "spouses," the ex-care subjects were more likely than the controls to have marked marital problems (28% v. 6%, $\chi^2 = 4.59$, 1 *df*, $p < .05$). Festinger reported marital satisfaction scores for her subjects that did not differ significantly from those derived from national population studies.

Parenting Outcomes Achieved

Ten of the 29 studies included data regarding their subjects' experiences as parents: Triseliotis and Russell [1984], Wolkind [1977a, 1977b], Meier [1965], Festinger [1983], Rest and Watson [1984], Zimmerman [1982], Frost and Jurich [1983], Jones and Moses [1984], and Cook et al. [1991]. One additional investigation, that of Quinton et al. [1986], focused specifically on parenting abilities. This last study was also the most rigorous of those that addressed parenting outcomes and will, therefore, be considered first and most extensively. This research, it will be remembered, involved a prospective comparison of women who had been in care in one of two British children's homes and women in the same geographic area who had never been in care.

Quinton et al. found that more of their subjects who had been in care had been pregnant than the control subjects (72% v. 43%, χ^2 = 8.50, 1 df, $p < .01$); and more of the ex-cares had been pregnant by age 19 (42% v. 5%, χ^2 = 16.75, 1 df, $p < .001$) and had a child (60% v. 36%, χ^2 = 5.85, 1 df, $p < .02$).

Quinton et al. noted that serious failures in parenting were evident only among the ex-care subjects. Nearly one-fifth of their children had been taken into placement in children's homes, and there was one case of infanticide. Eighteen percent (n = 5) of the ex-care subjects and none of the controls had children placed in care (Exact test $p = .075$). Thirty-five percent of the ex-cares (n = 10) and none of the controls had experienced some sort of transient or permanent parenting breakdown with at least one of their children (Exact test $p = .009$).

An overall assessment of parenting was completed for all subjects with children ages two or over; the assessment combined historical measures with an interview and observational measurement of current parental functioning. Because there were few control subjects with children at least two years old, the spouses of 14 males who had been in institutional care were added to this group; a comparison of these wives with the controls generally produced similar findings. The assessment yielded three levels of parental functioning: (1) *poor*—any children currently separated from their mothers because of parenting difficulties, marked lack of warmth shown to children, or low sensitivity to the children's needs, and difficulty in at least two out of the three areas of disciplinary control; (2) *intermediate*—no past history of parenting failure but some current problems, or vice versa; and (3) *good*—no mother-child separations of four weeks or more, no past history of parental breakdown, and no difficulty on any of the scales of current parental functioning.

The observational assessment of parenting in this study was based on seven different aspects of parenting: positive affect, negative affect, frequency of distress, frequency of control episodes, ignoring of child initiations, amount of child initiations, and amount of joint play. Thirty-five percent of the ex-cares and none of the controls fell into the lowest quartile on at least four of the seven areas; 11% of the ex-cares and 71% of the controls were in the top quartile on at least one parenting area; and 13% of the ex-cares and 48% of the controls showed no areas of difficulty ($\chi^2 = 11.746$, 2 *df*, $p < .005$).

In the overall assessment (historical, interview, and observational) of parental functioning, 51% of the ex-care subjects had a poor parental rating (including the 18% whose children were in family foster care or children's homes), as compared with 11% of the controls ($p < .01$). Twenty-three percent of the ex-cares and 48% of the controls had a *good* rating. This difference between the two groups remained even when the comparison was restricted to interviewer ratings of current parenting: 40% of the ex-cares and 11% of the controls were rated as poor ($\chi^2 = 6.91$, 2 *df*, $p < .05$); 31% of the ex-cares and 48% of the controls showed good current parenting.

The authors looked into the possibility that early pregnancies were related to parenting problems in the ex-care group and found that this factor did not explain the difference between the two groups; the difference remained when controlling for age at the time of the first pregnancy.

The impact on parenting of having a supportive spouse also was explored by Quinton et al. *Spouse* was defined as a man with whom the woman had a stable cohabitation of at least six months, such that the woman reported them as being an established couple with their own accommodation, though they were not necessarily legally married. The quality of parenting was significantly associated with the presence of a supportive spouse ($\chi^2 = 10.07$, 2 *df*, $p < .01$). Parenting was also associated with whether the spouse demonstrated psychosocial problems, including psychiatric disorders, criminality, chemical dependency, or long-standing problems in personal relationships ($\chi^2 = 14.53$, 2 *df*, $p < .001$). Half of the women with supportive spouses or spouses without psychosocial problems showed good parenting; this rate was as high as that in general population comparison groups.

The authors found that the ex-care mothers were more likely than the control mothers to be without a spouse (22% v. 0%), and the ex-care subjects as a whole (including those without children) were more likely than the controls to marry men with problems (51% v. 13 %, $\chi^2 = 11.32$, 1 *df*, $p < .001$).

The data led the authors to conclude that a spouse's good qualities exerted a "powerful ameliorating effect" leading to good parenting. It was clear that the ex-care females were less likely than the controls to have a supportive spouse (27% v. 74%).

In a British study that preceded Quinton et al., Wolkind [1977a; 1977b] compared primiparous women attending an obstetric clinic in London to determine the role of various background factors in predicting early pregnancy. Teen pregnancy was believed to be a risk factor in determining adequate maternal role functioning. Thirty-six of the 534 subjects in Wolkind's studies had been separated from their biological family for at least three months before age 16. Wolkind reports that the primiparous women who had reported having had a separation from their parent(s) during childhood were more likely to be in their teens than those who had not had a separation ($\chi^2 = 7.90$, 1 df, $p < .01$). Of those who had experienced a separation, the ones whose separations had occurred within a disrupted context, which included those who had been in care, were more likely to be under age 20 than those who had been separated in a stable context ($\chi^2 = 10.29$, 1 df, $p < .01$).

Three additional studies provide comparative data with regard to parenting outcomes. Festinger [1983] reported that similar percentages of women who had been in care as children and women in the general population had given birth by age 26. The more recent Westat study [Cook et al. 1991], however, employing a much larger sample than Festinger, strongly contradicts this finding. In the Westat study, 60% of the young women who had been in out-of-home care had given birth to a child by age 23 compared to only 24% of the women in general population of similar age range. The rate among youths formerly in care, was, however, nearly identical to the rate for young women in poverty in the general population.

Triseliotis and Russell [1984], in comparing adoptees with subjects who were placed in residential care, found no significant differences in overall birth rates or births to single mothers. Their sample, however, was small (21 married adoptees and 22 married subjects who had been in institutional-care), and their results may not generalize to the United States, since their study was conducted in Scotland.

All of Triseliotis and Russell's respondents reported having a close relationship with their children. The group that had been in institutional-care had more anxieties about parenting than did the adoptees; 45% of the former made references to difficulties or uncertainties about relating to their children. Subjects in the institutional-care group who were having difficulties with their own children were more likely to report that they had emotional problems during childhood ($p < .02$) and at the time of the interviews ($p < .0003$), that they had received psychological help within 12 months of the interviews ($p < .005$), and that they possessed a poor sense of well-being ($p < .006$). The lack of reported difficulties in parenting among the adoptees led the authors to conclude that a stable and caring environment after separating from parents can prevent a person from having problems as a parent later.

The remainder of the studies provide considerable descriptive data but no comparative data. An issue of particular interest concerning these subjects who had been in care is the need for placement of their own children in out-of-home care. While Festinger reported that all subjects with children were asked "whether any of the children had ever been placed in foster care or relinquished for adoption," it is difficult to ascertain the percentage who responded affirmatively to this question [1983: 139]. Festinger decided to exclude males from any analysis of this outcome, arguing that the data for males were flawed since "unmarried males sometimes were not, or perhaps could not be, as certain as females about such basic facts as birth" [1983: 140]. With regard to the females, she reported [1983: 144] that

> All but four of the 53 mothers were living with all of their children, and two of these four had at least one child with them.... Only one of the mothers had offspring in a foster home at the time of our contacts, although a few others had in previous years used foster care temporarily.

Twenty-nine percent of the males in Festinger's work had sired children, and about half of these were living with all of the children. Cook et al. [1991] reported a similar rate, with 24% of the males who had been in care having fathered a child.

The study conducted by Meier [1965] is of some interest because of the relatively older age of her subjects (28 to 32 years). This age range makes possible a better assessment of parenting capacity. Forty-one of the 42 women in Meier's study had given birth, for a combined total of 129 children. While it appears that the researcher knew which children were born to single mothers, the percentage of births to single mothers is not reported. Forty of the 41 women with children were caring for their children in their own homes (115 of the 129 children); one woman had lost custody of her two children when she was divorced; two children had died; and 10 children, born to seven single women, were in the care of another family, usually through adoption. Thus, in contrast to Festinger's findings with a relatively younger cohort, eight of the 41 women with children (20%) in Meier's study had had a child placed in out-of-home care.

Only one of the children born in wedlock had been placed in out-of-home care. Two mothers (with six children among them), however, were felt to be in precarious situations that could result in the use of out-of-home care in the future. On the whole, it was noted that the children looked happy, healthy, and well cared for. Meier reported that "most of these mothers *do* better than they *think they do*;" the mothers expressed more doubts about their role as mother than was warranted by the children's actual behavior [1965: 203 (emphasis in original)].

The Rest and Watson [1984] study has too few subjects to warrant attention here. Ferguson's [1966] prospective study achieved a very low attrition rate and provides good comparison data from other sources; the subjects, however, are relatively young at follow-up, making it difficult to assess parenting outcomes in terms of child placement. Ferguson did note that the 12% single-mother rate for 20-year-old females in his study compared with a rate of 6% for 22-year-old women in Glasgow in 1964.

The remaining three studies, all published between 1982 and 1984, are of similar design and quality. All employ retrospective designs without comparison groups and provide little if any comparative data from other sources. Findings from such studies are purely descriptive.

Forty-six percent of those who had been in care studied by Zimmerman [1982] study ($N = 170$) had children (25% of the men and 72% of the women). Of these, 36% lived with their children in a legal marriage, 14% lived with their children and their partner, 32% lived with their children alone or with extended family members, 7% had children who lived with a parent other than the interviewee, and 11% had children who lived with their grandparents. None of the children of the participants had been placed in out-of-home care.

Half of the children of the male subjects had been born out of wedlock. Five of the eight men with children were living with their children; two had children living with their ex-wives; and one had children living with their grandparents. All of the men reported that they saw and supported their children.

Of the 20 women with children, 30% were living with their husbands and children, 20% with their boyfriends and children, and 40% with their children alone or with extended family members. Zimmerman reported that all of the single-parent heads of households living with children were female (34% of the women and 16% of the total; in comparison, 41% of all African American women nationally were single parents in 1978).

Forty-six percent of the subjects reported that their children had some sort of problem in areas such as health, education, and behavior. The homes and quality of care of 17 subjects were evaluated; all of the children looked well cared for, but two parents lived in dangerous physical environments. Twenty-three percent of the parents reported grave concerns about meeting their children's physical needs; all of these parents lived below the poverty level. Twenty-seven percent of the parents said that they had grave concerns about their ability to provide adequate supervision for their children, to cope with their behavioral or emotional demands, or both.

Zimmerman categorized her participants into three groups, according to their individual functioning levels, as measured by their performance in three areas: adherence to the law, self-support, and caring for their own children. Sixty-seven percent were functioning at least adequately at the time of the study, while 33% were functioning inadequately in one or more basic areas of societal expectation. Subjects who had been married or divorced were functioning at a higher level than those who had never married ($p < .04$), and those who had common childbearing concerns were functioning better than those whose concerns were unusual or severe ($p < .02$).

Frost and Jurich [1983] found that 72% of their subjects had no children. More females than males had children (41% v. 19%). All of the women and 55% of the men with children lived with their offspring.

Jones and Moses [1984] reported that 43% of their female respondents, 13% of their male respondents, and 27% of their total subjects had at least one child. Nineteen percent of those with children reported that their child was in out-of-home care.

Extended Family Support Outcomes Achieved

Twelve studies described the adult relationships existing between former foster children and family members other than their spouses and children looking at relationships with biological parents, foster parents, biological siblings, and extended biological family members (Cook et al. [1991], Cook [1992], Triseliotis and Russell [1984], Harari [1980], Zimmerman [1982], Festinger [1983], Frost and Jurich [1983], Jones and Moses [1984], Ferguson [1966], Triseliotis [1980], Barth [1990], and Palmer [1976]). The findings are grouped by type of relationship.

BIOLOGICAL PARENTS. Relationships between adults who were in care as children and their biological parents have been of particular interest and are examined in 10 of the reviewed studies. Cook [1992] found that respondents to the national survey who had been in care had significantly less intimate relationships with both their fathers and mothers as compared to adults who had not been placed.

Triseliotis and Russell's study is particularly interesting in that it provides the only opportunity to compare subjects who spent extensive time as children in institutional care with subjects who were adopted. One-half of the institutional care subjects of Triseliotis and Russell's investigation had been in contact with at least one parent at some time after entering care. By comparison, 27% of the adopted subjects ($n = 44$) had established some form of contact with one or more members of their family of origin. Twenty percent of the institutional care subjects had frequent contact with one or both parent(s) at the time of the study, whereas only 7% (three of 44) of the adoptees had meaningful ongoing relationships with members of their biological families.

Most of the respondents who had been in institutional care felt forgiving and understanding toward their parents, assuming they had tried to cope but could not; one-quarter of them had negative feelings toward their parents for deserting or placing them. Those respondents who could remember life with their parents had few regrets about the separation. Of the institutional care group, however, 90% wished that some aspect of their past experiences would have been different; they most frequently regretted the lack of family life, poor relationships, the lack of information regarding their families, and the absence of contacts with the community. Most adoptees did not express interest in obtaining more information about their families of origin.

While the relatively closer ties with the biological family might appear positive for the institutional care group, it should be remembered from previous chapters that these ties have been found to be negatively associated with other adult outcomes. In general, the biological families of the subjects were probably ill-equipped to provide material and emotional support to their children.

Six retrospective studies of adults formerly in care as children provided additional descriptive information concerning relationships with biological parents (Harari [1980]; Zimmerman [1982]; Festinger [1983]; Frost and Jurich [1983]; Jones and Moses [1984]; and Cook et al. [1991]). With the exception of the Frost and Jurich study, the results of these surveys are quite similar. One-third to one-half of the subjects reported that they were in contact with their biological mothers and about one-fourth to one-third were in contact with their biological fathers. The Westat study [Cook et al. 1991] found that, when asked which two people had made the most difference in their lives, about one-fourth of the youths discharged from care identified their bioliogical or adoptive parents. Festinger provides the most detailed description and her results are quite close to those of Jones and Moses, Zimmerman, and Harari.

Eighty-three percent of the 186 subjects interviewed by Festinger were in touch with at least one member of their biological families. Over 48% maintained contact with their mothers, their fathers, or both; 22% had contact with their fathers and 36% with their mothers. Fifty-four percent were satisfied with the frequency of contact with their mothers, and 49% were satisfied with the frequency of contact with their fathers. Of those subjects who had stayed in touch with their biological parents or other nonsibling relatives, 38% felt "very close" to them, 33% felt "somewhat close," and the remainder felt "not very close" or "not close at all." Males tended to feel closer to these relatives than did females; 45% of the males and 28% of the females reported feeling "very close" to their blood relations.

Festinger also discovered that 167 of her 277 total participants had no contact at all with a particular family member. Thirty percent were satisfied with this situation, but 70% wanted contact. Of those desiring this additional contact, 34% wanted contact with their biological mothers, 70% with their biological fathers, and 46% with certain extended family members.

The contact rates reported by Frost and Jurich were considerably higher than those reported by Festinger. Frost and Jurich asked their subjects how much contact they had with members of their biological families. Forty-two percent had contact three to four times a week, 13% had contact on a weekly basis, 23% were in contact monthly, and 16% were in contact three to four times per year. Six percent had no contact with their biological families.

SIBLINGS. Fewer studies obtained information concerning relationships with biological siblings than studies concerned with biological families in general. The data that are available are purely descriptive. In general, it appears that sibling contact is much higher than contact with biological parents and, for many subjects, may be the only connection with the biological family.

Triseliotis and Russell [1984] reported that 33 of the 40 subjects who had been placed in residential establishments also had at least one sibling placed in the same facility; 90% of these described their relationship as very close. Many continued these close sibling relationships into adulthood; 41% had frequent contact with their siblings at the time of the study.

Festinger found that 12% of her subjects either had no siblings or else were not aware of having any. Of those with siblings that they knew, 72% had lived with one or more of them during their placements; and 92% had had contact with siblings during placement. At the time of the study, 44% were in touch with all of their known siblings, 9% had contact with none of them, and the remainder saw some but not all of their siblings.

Jones and Moses found that 82% of their respondents who had siblings were in contact with them at the time of the study—a much higher percentage than were in contact with biological parents.

Thirty-three of Harari's 34 subjects reported that they had siblings. Of these, 76% saw their siblings at least monthly, and 13% saw them about twice a year. Similarly, 85% of Zimmerman's respondents stated that they had contact at the time of the study with at least one sibling, and 19% had contact with all of them.

EXTENDED KIN. Forty-two percent of the 186 subjects interviewed by Festinger [1983] were in touch with a biological relative other than their parents or siblings. Fifty-nine percent of those who maintained contact were satisfied with the frequency of this contact. Cook et al. [1991] found that 54% of the youths in care they studied went to live with extended family members upon discharge and nearly 33% were still living with their extended family 2.5 to four years after discharge. For comparison, Cook et al. note that the majority of 18 to 24 year olds in the general population (52%) live with their parents or in a dormitory situation.

Jones and Moses [1984] reported that 35% of their respondents had contact with at least one relative other than their parents and siblings, while about half of Triseliotis and Russell's [1984] institutional care subjects had met such relatives. On the other hand, Harari [1980] indicated that few of her subjects had contact with extended family members.

Zimmerman [1982] asked her subjects formerly in care whom they currently felt closest to; 3% named their grandmothers. When asked with whom they felt kinship ties, 36% indicated their biological family, while 19% mentioned their in-laws; 13% named a combination of biological, foster, and in-law family members.

FOSTER FAMILIES. Harari [1980] suggested that her findings regarding foster family relationships should be interpreted with caution, for the subjects who agreed to participate often were located because their former foster parents knew and revealed their locations. This caution applies equally to all the retrospective studies, which constitute the bulk of the studies included in this review.

The one exception is the study by Ferguson [1966], which employed a prospective design and achieved a very low attrition rate; the subjects in this study, however, were quite young at follow-up (18 to 20 years old). Ferguson reported that at the time of follow-up, 27% of the male subjects and 34% of the females were living with their foster parents. Forty percent of the remaining males and 38% of the remaining females were in contact with their foster parents; 27% of the males and 23% of the females had no contact with members of their former foster families.

The retrospective studies, which used subjects who were somewhat older than those in other studies, reported varying percentages of subjects who were still living with foster parents at the time of the study. Cook et al. [1991] found that only 10% of their subjects remained with their foster parents after discharge and 2.5 to four years later, only 5% were living with them. Festinger's rate at the time of the interview was also low (12%). Harari, however, reported that 21% of those studied had never left the family foster home after discharge or had returned to there. Triseliotis reported that 35% were living with foster parents and considered the foster parents to be their family.

Clearly, foster parents remain important resources long after discharge. Both Barth [1990] and Festinger [1983] report that 89% of their subjects reported some contact with their foster or group-home parents since leaving care. Festinger found that 89% of those maintaining contact with their foster family had frequent contact. Of those who maintained contact with their last foster family, most felt very close to them.

Fifty-seven percent of Harari's [1980] subjects who had not continued to live with their last foster parents felt that they could count on them for support, while 27% felt they could not count on them, and 16% were uncertain. The perceived absence of support usually centered on money or other concrete issues. Of those respondents who had more than one foster home, 32% maintained contact with a foster parent other than the last one.

Palmer [1976] asked her respondents about the level of identification they felt with their foster families; identification was defined as feelings of belonging or affection. The majority indicated that they felt a positive identification. Respondents seemed to identify more positively with foster families than with their biological families. The levels of identification subjects felt with foster families and biological families were found to be independent; one did not necessarily rise as the other fell. Festinger reported similar findings in this regard.

Jones and Moses [1984] found that during the first year after discharge, excluding those subjects who continued to live with their foster families, 77% of the respondents had contact with their former foster parents. At the time they responded to the questionnaire, 72% of the subjects who had foster parents were in contact with them; this contact typically occurred at least weekly. Thirty-eight percent were in contact with other people who, as children, had lived in the foster home. Forty-four percent of the respondents who had lived in group or institutional placements had contact with staff members from those settings. Triseliotis and Russell [1984] reported similar findings for subjects who had been in institutional care.

Social Support Outcomes Achieved

Eleven studies provide descriptive information concerning the subject's general ability to establish and maintain relationships including friendships, involvement in organizations, and leisure-time activities, but only four of which offer comparative data. The eleven studies are: Cook [1992], Cook et al. [1991], Quinton et al. [1986], Triseliotis and Russell [1984],

Festinger [1983], Maas [1963], Allerhand et al. [1966], Harari [1980], Zimmerman [1982], Frost and Jurich [1983], and Jones and Moses [1984].

Three of the four studies providing comparative data found social support to be lacking for adults who had been in out-of-home care. While Quinton et al. [1986] found that the ex-care subjects were more likely to report poor social relationships than the controls (18% v. 10%), these results were not statistically significant given the relatively small sample size (N = 145). Similarly, compared to 16% of the adoptees, 28% of the institutional care subjects in the Triseliotis and Russell study [1984] reported having moderate to severe difficulties making friends and mixing. In her analysis of data from the 1988 National Survey of Families and Households, Cook [1992] found that children formerly in care scored significantly higher on levels of social isolation than adults who had never been in out-of-home care.

Festinger again provides rich descriptive data, which she compares to results for the general population. In general, her results seem to contradict the findings of the three comparison studies cited above. Ninety-six percent of Festinger's subjects felt that there was someone to whom they could turn for help or advice, and 22% (more females than males) felt there were many such people in their lives. Thirty percent of the respondents were uncertain precisely whom they could count on for help. Those who had been in care were similar to the general population comparison group in the number of people they felt they could count on for help. However, the group that had been in care disagreed less than did the general population with the statement that "These days I really know whom I can count on for help."

Roughly 10% of Festinger's subjects (14% of the males and 6% of the females) felt that "no one cares much what happens to me;" African Americans formerly in care disagreed with this statement less than did the general African American population. Festinger also reports that Caucasians in the out-of-home care and general population surveys had the same alienation scores; African Americans had higher alienation scores than Caucasians in both samples. Females who had been in out-of-home care felt less alienated than females in the general population.

Forty-two percent of Festinger's respondents belonged to formal organizations, and all were pleased with their experiences in these groups; this level of involvement was similar to that found in the national general population survey used for comparison. Ten percent of the subjects attended religious services at least once a week, and an additional 42% attended infrequently; one-third never attended services, and 15% claimed no affiliation with a formal religion. Most were satisfied with their religion: 62% expressed some, much, or very much satisfaction in this area. Festinger stated that the percentage of her subjects with a religious preference and the frequency of attendance at services were comparable to the figures from the general population survey.

Festinger also found that most of her subjects had four to five close friends; 65% of these had met some of their friends while in out-of-home care. Seven percent of the respondents had no close friends, 37% wanted more friends, and one-quarter wished that people liked them more. She noted that her findings were similar to those of national general population surveys in the level of satisfaction with friends, the number of friends, the frequency of contact with close friends, and the number who wished that people liked them more.

Most of Festinger's subjects were reasonably satisfied with their neighbors and knew one or more of them, although one-quarter of them had no contact with their neighbors. This data was comparable to that obtained in national surveys.

The remainder of the studies (Maas [1963]; Allerhand et al. [1966]; Harari [1980]; Zimmerman [1982]; Frost and Jurich [1983]; and Jones and Moses [1984]), which do not provide a basis for comparison, seem to agree that the majority of subjects have reasonable social support systems. Participation in groups is also high but not as high as other indicators of social support used. The lowest rate of group participation was noted by Jones and Moses. Only 30% of their respondents belonged to any group, and three-quarters of these were religiously based. Seventy-eight percent had a religious preference, and significantly more women than men expressed a preference ($p = .05$); 61% attended religious services, and 76% stated that church was important to them.

Taken together, these findings suggest that the majority of children formerly in care are able to form social relationships as adults and that they find these relationships generally fulfilling. A significant minority, however, struggle in this area, and, Festinger's results notwithstanding, subjects who have been in care appear to be at greater risk of poor social support and relationships than those who have not, as evidenced by the findings of the rigorous studies of Quinton et al. [1986] and Triseliotis and Russell [1984].

Family and Social Support: An Outcomes Summary and Predictors

Findings with regard to the ability of children formerly in care to secure family and social support as adults are far from conclusive. Results from two of the better-designed studies that also provide a direct comparison group [Quinton et al. 1986; Triseliotis & Russell 1984] suggest that problems may exist in forming stable cohabiting partnerships, in fulfilling parenting roles, and in achieving integrated and supportive social relationships in the community. These risks seem to be heightened for males [Cook et al. 1991], when the child's path that leads to later entry into care [Fanshel & Shinn 1978; Festinger 1983; Jones & Moses 1984], when children have greater social and behavioral problems [Triseliotis & Russell 1984], when placement is in group settings [Festinger 1983; Triseliotis & Russell 1984], and in cases of reunification with and emotional rejection by the biological family [Palmer 1976;

Zimmerman 1982]. As adults, these individuals are more likely to experience teen pregnancies, marriages with a non-supportive spouse, and greater social isolation than their peers in the general population.

On the other hand, additional findings from these and other studies suggest that these risks may be ameliorated through nurturing and stable family foster care and adoption arrangements [Festinger 1983; Triseliotis & Russell 1984; Triseliotis 1980; Zimmerman 1982]. Long-term and stable placements were found to be associated with greater identification with the foster family and improved parenting outcomes as adults [Festinger 1983; Jones & Moses 1984; Palmer 1976; Zimmerman 1982].

Chapter 8

Personal Well-Being

The final set of outcomes reflects the personal well-being of those who were in out-of-home care as children. This chapter describes findings on physical health, mental health, and general well-being or life satisfaction.

Physical Health Outcomes Achieved

Less attention has been paid by researchers to this outcome area than to those discussed earlier in this book. Only eight of the 29 studies of those in care as children included data related to the subject's physical health as adults and, even within these studies, the topic receives minimal consideration. The studies are Wolkind [1976a, 1976b], Triseliotis and Russell [1984], Festinger [1983], Cook et al. [1991], Ferguson [1966], Barth [1990], Jones and Moses [1984], and Zimmerman [1982].

Wolkind's study is one of two that include a comparison group, but the out-of-home care group contains only 36 subjects. The pregnant women who participated in this study were administered the Malaise Inventory, a questionnaire derived from the Cornell Medical Index, which pertains to a woman's usual health before pregnancy. The subjects who admitted to having been separated from their parents during childhood had significantly higher Malaise scores, indicating poorer health, than did those who were not separated ($t = 5.05$, $p < .001$). In the first group, those whose separations had occurred within a disrupted context had higher Malaise scores than those whose separations had occurred within a stable context ($t = 2.33$, 102 df, $p < .05$).

Wolkind found that, among these same subjects, those who had been in out-of-home care were more likely to describe their health as having deteriorated since pregnancy (31% v. 13%, $\chi^2 = 7.05$, 1 df, $p < .01$) and to have had higher mean scores on the Malaise Inventory (6.26 v. 3.82, $t = 4.43$, $p < .001$).

Triseliotis and Russell [1984] found no difference between the adoptees and those who received residential care in their study of Scottish subjects. In general, both groups of subjects considered themselves less healthy than did the subjects of the other investigations reported in this book. Seventy percent rated their health as *good*, and all except one of the others described their health as *average*; the health of one subject who had been in care was described as *poor*.

The Festinger [1983] and Ferguson [1966] studies do not include a control group but do provide comparative data from other sources; both have relatively large samples. Festinger's retrospective design, however, results in a significant dropout rate and possible sample bias. Ferguson's study employs a prospective approach with very little attrition.

Ferguson questioned his Scottish subjects about their history of work days missed owing to illness. Between the ages of 18 and 20, his subjects had missed fewer days of work as a result of illness than had the general population of the same age; only "two or three" of the 203 subjects had lost work time.

Of Festinger's New York City respondents, 79% reported having no particular physical or health troubles. Almost 85%

described their health as excellent or good, and 2% described it as poor. Of the 21% who reported health problems, the severity of those problems ranged from serious to minor. There was no difference in the self-assessment of overall health between the children formerly in care (1975 cohort) and the general population of the country. These two groups did differ, however, on two particular symptoms: Caucasians who had been in care had fewer upset stomachs than Caucasians in the general population; and African Americans who had been in care and Caucasians who had been placed in group homes had more nightmares than the general population.

Festinger's subjects, discharged from care in 1975, reported health status information similar to that reported by the comparison subjects who had been discharged in 1970. The 1970 cohort differed from the general population on one dimension: Caucasians who had been in care had fewer health complaints than the general population sample. Festinger concluded that, overall, those who had been in care and the population in general were similar with respect to their health and symptomatology.

Barth's [1990] subjects reported more health problems than Festinger's subjects. Forty-four percent had had a "serious illness or accident" since leaving care, with about one-fourth (24% of the sample) requiring hospitalization. Slightly more than half (53%) rated their health as very good or excellent.

Jones and Moses [1984] and Cook et al. [1991] reported rates of health problems quite similar to Festinger's; neither study, however, provides comparison data for this variable. Cook et al. also reported that 65% of the youths indicated that they had always been able to get health care when needed since discharge from care.

Finally, Zimmerman's [1982] retrospective survey does provide comparison data for this outcome area. Twenty-nine percent of the respondents rated their health as fair or poor, compared with 12% of the general population. Zimmerman points out, however, that the discrepancy between the two rates is probably less dramatic than it appears. Within the general population, 26% of those with incomes of less than $5,000 and 17% of those with incomes between $5,000 and $9,000 rated their health as fair or poor; 36% of Zimmerman's subjects reported incomes of $5,000 or less, and 25% reported incomes between $5,000 and $9,000. These findings seem to indicate that health status may be influenced more directly by income than by a history of placement in care.

Adults who experienced out-of-home care may indeed have poorer health than the general population, but their health status may be quite similar to that of other low-income populations. The scarcity of information on this outcome suggests the need for more research.

Mental Health Outcomes Achieved

Mental health is a widely studied outcome, with 13 different studies reporting findings in this area of functioning (Cook [1992]; Robins [1966]; Quinton et al. [1986]; Heston et al. [1966]; Wolkind [1977a, 1977b]; Triseliotis & Russell [1984]; Barth [1990]; Harari [1980]; Zimmerman [1982]; Festinger [1983]; Palmer [1976]; Fanshel & Shinn [1978]; and Maas [1963]). These include five of the better-designed studies reviewed, those of Robins, Quinton et al., Heston et al., Wolkind, and Triseliotis and Russell; however, all but Robins' study were conducted outside the United States.

Although Robins' study is dated, it is one of the best designed of the 29 studies included in this review. In addition, its major focus was the mental health of the subjects. Robins compared 524 former patients at child guidance clinics with 100 nonpatient subjects for the purpose of describing the "natural history" of the sociopathic personality [1966: 1]. Of the former child guidance patients, 28% of the males and 47% of the females had lived in an institution or family foster home by the time they were referred for care. The author found that the proportion of these subjects later diagnosed as having a sociopathic personality did not vary significantly with the type of out-of-home care received; children raised by both parents, however, were more often well than other children ($p < .05$), and children for whom parents did not have legal responsibility were least often well.

Those with a diagnosis of schizophrenia had a higher rate of removal from their homes as children because of parental neglect than did the well group (35% v. 7%). More females with a diagnosis of hysteria than well females had been wards of the state (25% v. 0%); 85% of those with hysteria, compared to 42% of the well females, had lived away from their parents at some time ($p < .05$).

A second methodologically sound study—Quinton et al. [1986]—also examined the mental health of study subjects. The findings of this study and those reported 20 years earlier by Robins are in agreement. Quinton et al. reported that while in care and at follow-up, those British female subjects who had been residents of Children's Homes evidenced greater mental disturbance than members of the control group. At the time of follow-up, those who had been in care were more likely than the controls to have a current psychiatric disorder (31% v. 5%, $\chi^2 = 9.21$, 1 df, $p < .01$). They also were more likely to have a personality disorder, as evidenced by persisting handicaps in interpersonal relationships since their early teens or earlier (25% v. 0%, $\chi^2 = 10.37$, 1 df, $p < .01$).

Three additional studies that examined mental health status also included control groups. Of these three studies, Heston et al. [1966] found no differences between groups. Two, Wolkind [1977a, 1977b] and Triseliotis and Russell [1984], found those who had been in care to be doing worse than the controls.

Wolkind discovered that women who admitted to a separation from one or more of their parents during childhood were more likely than others in the study to have seen a psychiatrist or to have received psychotropic drugs from general practitioners ($\chi^2 = 3.98$, 1 *df*, *p* < .05).

Triseliotis and Russell defined as "disturbed" those subjects who possessed two or more of the following four characteristics: (1) serious relationship problems with marital partners and friends, (2) psychiatric referral in adult life, (3) heavy drinking or drug use, and (4) a criminal record, excluding automobile offenses. Significantly more of the institutional care group compared to the adoptees were classified as disturbed (38% v. 16%); one adoptee and seven institutional care subjects met three or more of the criteria.

Five additional studies provided comparative data or used standardized tests to judge the mental health status of children formerly in care. Cook [1992] found subjects formerly in care to have significantly higher depression and lower self-esteem scores than those who had not been in out-of-home care placements even after controlling for socioeconomic and demographic variables. Barth [1990] found that the mean score for his subjects on the Center for Epidemiologic Studies Depression Scale (CES-D) was 36, which is higher than the cutoff score used to indicate the presence of depression. Harari [1980] used the Jackson Personality Inventory (JPI) as an adjustment measurement. According to Harari, mean scores for self-esteem (males, 12.87, and females, 11.81) and for interpersonal affect (males, 10.87, and females, 14.46) "compare favorably with JPI normative samples" (1980: 182). Zimmerman [1982] reported that the rate of mental health problems seemed to be similar to that found among low-income people in the general population.

Festinger [1983], however, found that more of those who had been in care as children had turned to mental health professionals for help than did individuals in the general population. Since leaving care, 47% of Festinger's respondents had gone to a professional for advice or counsel with personal problems. The most-used sources of counseling were clergy

(19%) and social agencies (16%), usually the agency which had discharged the subject. Fifteen percent of those formerly in care had used more than one source of help. Thirty percent of the subjects—38% of the women and 25% of the men—had used mental health and social agency contacts. Most who sought assistance felt they had been helped.

Of the remaining three studies that provide results bearing on mental health status, two, Palmer [1976] and Fanshel & Shinn [1978], do not provide data on the adult functioning of their subjects. Under the conceptual framework of this review, however, mental health status while in care and at discharge is considered to be a possible predictor of adult outcomes and is discussed in Chapter 9, which describes factors associated with mental health outcomes.

The earliest report to address the issue of mental health is that of Maas [1963], who retrospectively studied 20 young adults who, as preschool children in London during World War II, had been placed for their safety by their parents in British wartime residential nurseries. Maas sought to determine whether the subjects suffered "irreversible psychosocial damage" as a result of their separation from their families. Given the date of this study, its location, and the peculiar situation surrounding the placement of the children, it is not clear that its findings should be generalized or compared with those of other studies. The internal validity of this study also suffers from the small sample size, lack of a comparison group, and questionable selection criteria. It will only be noted here that Maas concluded that "at least from about age two, early childhood separation and preschool residential care are not themselves *sufficient* antecedents to a seriously troubled or troublesome young adulthood."

Life Satisfaction Achieved

Seven studies examined overall life satisfaction outcome: Triseliotis [1980]; Triseliotis and Russell [1984]; Festinger

[1983]; Zimmerman [1982]; Jones and Moses [1984]; Cook et al. [1991]; and Cook [1992]. Of these studies, the work of Triseliotis, and of Triseliotis and Russell, provide the most direct comparative data. Triseliotis and Russell reported that about 90% of their adopted subjects and 60% of those who had been in institutional care rated their feelings of well-being as good or very good, while the remainder rated their feelings as uncertain or poor. Sixty-one percent of the adoptees and 20% of the institutional care group indicated that they were very happy with their present lives; 32% of the former and 47% of the latter stated that they were fairly happy.

These results can be compared with those from the 1980 study by Triseliotis, which focused exclusively on family foster home subjects. In that study, he found that 24 of his respondents (60%) felt satisfied with themselves and with their lives; they had strong positive self-images and most were satisfied with their growing-up experience. Six (15%) had some reservations about themselves, and 10 (25%) felt dissatisfied with their lives and pessimistic about their futures. They attributed their negative self-images to having been in care.

Festinger compared her findings regarding both the 1970 and 1975 samples of New York City former foster children with the findings of several general-population studies: a well-being study conducted at the Institute for Social Research of the University of Michigan, general population data for New York City, and national surveys conducted by the National Opinion Research Center at the University of Chicago.

For those respondents who had been discharged from care in 1975, Festinger found that, with regard to self-esteem, Caucasians who had been placed in family foster homes reported findings similar to those in the general population; Caucasians who had lived in group settings compared less favorably to those in the general population. Her African American respondents scored a little lower than the national subjects on the statement "I am a person of worth"; they had similar responses, however, to other self-esteem questions, leading Festinger to conclude that their level of self-esteem was essentially the same as that of African Americans in the general population. As a whole, her subjects were similar to those in the other out-of-home care studies described here in their sense of happiness and their satisfaction with life as a whole, except that the Caucasians who had lived in group settings scored lower than those placed in family foster care on both of these measures.

When Festinger compared those who had been discharged from family foster care in 1970 with the general population, she found very few differences. Although no significant difference was found between the two groups in their sense of well-being, Caucasians who had lived in family foster homes expressed more dissatisfaction with "life in the U.S. today."

In comparing subjects discharged in 1975 with those discharged in 1970, Festinger found that the older group felt less alienated. She suggested that this was not unusual, because younger adults generally have less employment security and lower earnings than older ones, and the change to independent living was more recent for the former. The older respondents expressed more satisfaction with "life in the U.S. today," but the groups were similar with regard to feelings of well-being and optimism. Festinger concluded that "no harmful effects [of out-of-home care] emerged with the passing years. If anything, they seemed more settled and in control of various aspects of their lives than those who were more recently discharged" [1983: 228].

Cook [1992] also found no significant differences in life happiness when comparing adults who had been in care as children with other adults responding to the 1988 National Survey of Families and Households.

The remaining three studies (Cook et al. [1991]; Zimmerman [1982]; and Jones and Moses [1984]) were purely descriptive, and the form in which the results were presented does not permit comparison with Festinger's results. The results of two studies, however, do appear to be in close agreement with each other, reporting that between 15% and 17% of their subjects were dissatisfied or unhappy [Jones & Moses 1984; Zimmerman 1982].

It is difficult, and perhaps ill-advised, to try to form any opinions based on these sparse and conflicting findings. The Scottish studies and the U.S. study by Festinger do, however, suggest that subjects from group care settings fare more poorly in the area of life satisfaction than do adoptees, those from family foster homes, and the general population.

Personal Well-Being: An Outcomes Summary and Predictors

Relatively little research has been done on the effects of out-of-home care on the adult outcome of physical health, making it impossible to draw conclusions or to even speculate about associations. Several predictors of life satisfaction and general sense of well-being have been identified, however, for persons formerly in care. The following subjects seem to fare better: those placed in family foster homes rather than group or institutional settings [Festinger 1983; Triseliotis & Russell 1984; Triseliotis 1980]; those who are placed at younger ages [Festinger 1983; Jones & Moses 1984], in stable homes, and for longer periods of time [Cook 1992; Jones & Moses 1984]; and those who graduate from high school before discharge and those who maintain contact with their foster family after leaving care [Festinger 1983; Jones & Moses 1984].

More attention has been paid to mental health outcomes, and the results suggest that subjects who spent time in care fare poorly in this area. Contrary to other findings, type of placement is not a consistent predictor of mental health; nor is age at placement [Festinger 1983; Palmer 1976; Robins 1966]. Contact with the biological family was not found to be associated with better mental health outcomes, although increased contact with siblings was [Festinger 1983; Palmer 1976]. School performance was also found to be a positive predictor of adult mental health outcomes [Festinger 1983]. Overall, however, it appears that the incidence of mental health problems is relatively stable and that the best predictor of problems in adulthood is the presence of emotional or behavioral problems as a child [Fanshel & Shinn 1978; Festinger 1983; Triseliotis & Russell 1984].

IV: Summary and Conclusions

Chapter 9

Outcomes Achieved

One may be easily tempted to skip the prior chapters of this book and turn only to these summary chapters, which attempt to pull the fragmentary findings noted earlier together into a coherent picture. The reader, however, is strongly cautioned against such an approach. This summary of findings and the conclusions in the next chapter reflect the variations in the quality of the studies reviewed. The studies vary according to dates conducted, geographic location, sample size, attrition rates, and their inclusion of comparison groups. Just as is evident in the summation below, some findings involve substantial ranges. The earlier chapters of this book provide the context within which the findings of this chapter are to be considered. That context involves an understanding of the strengths and limitations of each of the studies as well as the basis on which those strengths and limitations have been determined. As the authors have attempted to do, readers are encouraged to weigh such factors carefully in their appraisal of adult outcomes for former foster children.

Adult Self-Sufficiency

One of the most important functions of the foster care system is to prepare for independent living those individuals who age out of the system. The ability of individuals to be self-sufficient has much to do with their employability (or the employability of a spouse), which is, at least in part, a function of education. So for both individuals who leave the system to live independently as adults and those who leave the system to return home or go to other living arrangements, the most basic level of achievement is the eventual completion of high school. In their national evaluation of independent living programs, Cook et al. [1991] found that completion of high school before discharge consistently led to better adult outcomes, regardless of skills training.

Unfortunately, the studies reviewed here reveal that somewhere between 15% and 56% of those formerly placed in out-of-home care as children did not complete high school or earn a GED, a rate which is higher than that found among individuals who were not in care as children. Adoptees were more likely to finish school than individuals who had been in residential care, who in turn were more likely to finish high school than those who had been in family foster homes. Triseliotis and Russell [1984] suggested that the low rates of completion for family foster care subjects may have reflected the foster parents' expectations. The median educational level attained by children formerly in care for the studies reported here ranged between 9 and 11.5 years, approximately one year below the average level for the general population. This difference was reduced when those formerly in out-of-home care as children were compared to other children from low-income families. A few studies revealed that 8% to 40% of subjects had earned some college credit.

The school performance of individuals with a history of foster placement was below average and below their capacities, with substantial numbers of individuals behind their age-appropriate grade level, and with 20% to 50% having repeated a grade or grades in school. Fanshel et al. [1990] found that placement in care did not compensate for educational deficits: those behind at the time of placement were still behind at the time of discharge. One-third to one-half of the subjects who were asked expressed regrets about not achieving a higher educational level while in care, and they rated educational counseling as one of the three most important areas for agencies to stress in discharge planning.

Fifteen studies provided some measure of employment or self-sufficiency. Given the above educational outcomes, it is somewhat surprising that unemployment among those formerly in out-of-home care did not differ from rates in the general population. Unemployment rates for the respondents in the various studies ranged from 19% to 50%, the latter a finding in a sample of individuals formerly in a residential institution. A majority of those formerly in care as children were self-supporting (52% to 92%), although some had received public assistance at some point in their adult lives (4% to 50%). Again, those discharged from group homes or institutions had higher rates of public assistance than men and women their age in the general population of New York City. Despite similar employment rates, subjects formerly in care as children often had unskilled or semiskilled jobs without security, similar to the jobs held by their parents. There appears to have been little upward mobility.

Twelve studies examined the housing of sample members. Individuals who had been separated from their families were more likely to live in poor housing than individuals who had not lived apart. Most people, however, were satisfied with their current housing. A majority of those formerly in care as children were living independently, either alone or with a spouse. In those studies involving younger adults, roughly 20% were living with former foster parents or members of their biological family. One-half of the respondents, when asked in one investigation, reported that they had received either little or no preparation for discharge into independent living. Moves from one location to another occurred more often for former foster children than for people in the general population. One study [Harari 1980] reported an average of 3.9 moves for subjects who had left care one to five years earlier.

Several studies of homeless persons have now revealed that a disproportionate number of them spent some time in out-of-home care during their childhood. Six of these studies were discussed in detail in Chapter 4. The proportion of homeless persons who reported they were in out-of-home placement as children ranges from 15% to 39%. Among a sample of psychiatric patients, those formerly in care were much more likely to experience homelessness as adults, even after controlling for age, ethnicity, gender, psychiatric diagnosis, and history of substance abuse.

Researchers have been quick to point out, however, that the process by which childhood placement and adult homelessness are linked is not yet clear. It may be that the children came into care with severe problems, or that care created personal problems for them. Another possibility is that care was necessary because of family difficulties, and placement functioned to further weaken family ties that would have helped individuals avoid homelessness in adulthood. There is also growing recognition of the failure of the out-of-home care system to adequately prepare persons for independent living.

While it seems clear that those formerly in care as children are at increased risk of welfare dependency and homelessness, it should be noted that the majority have been able to provide for themselves for the most part, with only occasional governmental financial assistance. For many, this is in spite of poor academic performance, the failure to complete high school, and perhaps most important, the failure to receive adequate preparation for independent living. However, these shortcomings place them at high risk for losing their tenuous grip on self-sufficiency.

Behavioral Adjustment

Investigators have examined both crime and substance abuse among those formerly in care. Eleven studies provided information regarding criminal behavior. Mirroring the general population, arrest rates for females (5% to 10%) are lower than the rates for males (25% to 40%). Those males who were formerly in placement appear to engage in crime more often than similarly aged males in the general population. For those males who were in placement, 22% to 33% were convicted of crimes; incarceration rates ranged from 14% to 22%.

The evidence regarding substance use among those formerly in care is mixed. Frequency and quantity of alcohol use appear to be higher among former foster children than the general population. In one study [Festinger 1983] 29% of males and 12% of females reported drinking at least three times per week; blacks in the out-of-home care group drank "too much" more often than blacks in the general population.

Drug use appeared to be high and on the rise for children formerly in care, as it is in the general population. Twenty-nine percent of the males and 14% of the females reported having used at least one drug practically every day.

It should not be too surprising that rates of criminal behavior and chemical dependency would be higher among those formerly in care. Both conditions have been noted as responses to poverty, and those formerly in care often come from poor families and live in poverty themselves. Future investigations of criminal behavior and chemical dependency among those once in care need to separate the effect of poverty from that of childhood placement.

Family and Social Support

The connections maintained by those formerly in out-of-home care to family and other social supports are of particular interest to researchers. Families and others serve to buffer the effects of life's difficult problems. Separation from family members may not only cut off potential support, but it may also stunt a person's ability to form supportive relationships in other contexts. Further, the ability to form and maintain family and interpersonal relationships provides a strong measure of individual functioning.

In 14 studies which examined marriage rates, the mean median rate was 30%, with a range of 13% to 93%. The variation is a function, in part, of the differences in ages of subjects across studies as well as the time since discharge from foster care. The 93% rate was for a study with the oldest subjects and longest period since care. Nonetheless, comparative investigations showed that marriage rates for those formerly in care were substantially lower than those for the general population and for individuals who had not been separated from their parents. This was true even when investigators included cohabiting relationships.

Divorce rates did not appear to differ, although people who had been in care were more likely to have substantial difficulties in sexual or love relationships, and women were more likely to have married men with personal problems (psychiatric, criminal, relational, and alcohol and drug). Marital satisfaction was not found to vary, however, between those who had experienced out-of-home care and those who had not. Ninety percent of respondents reported being very happy or pretty happy with their partners, a percentage that did not differ significantly from that found in national population studies.

As parents, adults who were formerly in care were significantly different from those not in care as children. A common research bias was to focus on the women as parents; thus, most findings, with a few exceptions as noted, pertain to women. Researchers found separation from family to be linked to early pregnancies, and most respondents indicated they wished they had been older when their first child was born. One study [Ferguson 1966] which examined nonmarital birthrates in Glasgow, Scotland, found a rate of 11.5% for women formerly in care compared to a 6% rate for similarly aged women. In their more recent study, Cook et al. [1991] found that 60% of the young women who had been in out-of-home care had given birth to a child within 2.5 to 4 years after discharge. Becoming a young mother was associated with becoming a cost to the community after discharge from care.

While most women had children and were currently living with them, some reported that one or more of their children had been placed out of the home at some time (19% of women in one study). The women who had been in out-of-home care as children were more likely to have been pregnant, to have been pregnant at an earlier age, and to exhibit serious failures in their parenting than control subjects. Based on the infrequency of parenting difficulties among a comparison group of adoptees, one researcher concluded a stable and caring environment after separation from one's family can ameliorate the effects of that separation on parenting abilities. Those women who had never married were more likely to be functioning inadequately than those who had been married or divorced. In one study the quality of parenting was associated with the presence or absence of a supportive spouse and the presence or absence of psychosocial problems in the spouse. Unfortunately, those women who had been in care were less likely than the controls to have a spouse and to have one without problems.

Men who had been in care were less likely to have children than women and less likely to be living with them [Frost & Jurich 1983; Cook et al. 1991]. Eighty-eight percent of the men rated themselves as excellent or good parents, similar to the 81% for women [Frost & Jurich 1983].

It appears that separation from one's family in childhood does not result in separation from that family in adulthood. About half of the studies examined this issue. A majority of those formerly in care reported that they were in contact with at least one biological family member: 82% to 94%. Two-thirds indicated they felt very close or somewhat close to their biological relatives. Contact with siblings was reportedly higher than contact with biological parents; about one-half reported current contact with mothers, one-third with fathers, and about 90% with at least one sibling.

Foster families apparently provide a great deal of affiliation for former foster children in their early adult years. Respondents reported high rates of contact with former foster parents: 63% to 89% had contact with at least one foster family member. Researchers reported that 12% to 35% of subjects were still living with their foster families. A majority of respondents reported that they felt they could count on their foster parents for support. Palmer [1976] found that respondents seemed to identify more positively with foster families than with their biological families. These results must be interpreted with caution, however, since in most studies, some of the subjects were located through their former foster families.

Respondents even continued contact with staff members from residential settings. In one study, 44% reported contact with a staff member since discharge [Jones & Moses 1984], and in another study 60% of those who had been in institutions indicated that they felt close or very close to their former houseparents [Triseliotis & Russell 1984].

The majority of those formerly in care seem to have reasonable social support systems. Nine studies provided information on this area. Those placed in care as children were comparable to the general population in their number of friends, frequency of contact, level of satisfaction with friends, and familiarity with their neighbors. Some individuals did report poor social relationships (18%) and moderate to severe difficulties in making friends and mixing with others. Once again, the variation was greatest between those subjects who experienced institutional care and those who were adopted. Most respondents identified four to five close friends, with only 7% indicating they had no close friends. These findings are similar to those for the national general population. Festinger [1983] noted that 42% of the sample belonged to formal organizations, also similar to figures for the general population. A majority of those formerly in care stated a preference for religion and reported a frequency of attendance that was also comparable to the general population.

It does not appear that adults once in care as children have been rendered incapable of maintaining relationships with their biological families or of establishing relationships with others. Further, they find these relationships fulfilling. The fact that many more were able to maintain contact with their biological siblings than with their parents speaks to the importance of maintaining sibling units together in placements.

Personal Well-Being

Physical health, mental health, and life satisfaction are areas of personal well-being, some of which have been assessed by investigators of those placed in care as children. Conclusions are difficult to draw from the mixed findings of the limited number of studies that examined physical health. Several studies, however, suggest that when compared to the general population, those formerly in care as children generally have poorer mental health, and those who were placed in group settings rather than family foster homes score lower on various measures of life satisfaction.

Eight studies of the adult health of those formerly in care as children have been conducted. Three of those studies suggest that adults once in care as children have poorer physical health than the general population, a difference that, though reduced, seems to hold even after controlling for income. In those three studies, 15% to 30% of subjects reported their health as fair or poor, compared to about 12% of subjects in comparison groups. Roughly a fifth of those formerly in care as children report having a health problem as an adult, and this rate seems to be higher among those who resided in group settings. A study completed in the 1960s, however, found that those individuals who had been in care missed fewer work days due to illness than those of the same age in the general population. One other study found no differences between the subjects formerly in care as children and the general population. The other studies reporting health status provided no comparison data.

Mental health was the most widely studied outcome for those formerly in care. Because of the drastically varying measures of mental health used in the 13 research studies that examined this area, however, it is difficult to say anything beyond the general finding that adults formerly in care as children seem as adults to exhibit problems in the area of mental health. They were more likely to be referred to and use psychiatrists than were adoptees or persons in the general population. In addition, current psychiatric disorders were more prevalent among those formerly in care both as adults and as children compared to study controls, although at least one study [Hesten et al. 1966] did not find any differences.

Individuals who had been in a foster family did not differ from adoptees in their satisfaction with life, but those who had been in group settings did. Adoptees and foster family subjects more often reported well-being and happiness with life than did those from institutions. Individuals from group settings, particularly Caucasians, reported less self-esteem, happiness, and satisfaction with life on a whole than did those who grew up in foster families and persons in the general population.

What is interesting about the findings regarding personal well-being is that in spite of possibly poorer physical health and tentative indications of more difficulties in the area of mental health, those formerly in care did not see life as any less satisfying than adults who were never separated from their families as children. This may speak to how people form expectations or the tendency of people to adapt to their situations.

If, then, these are the outcomes for adults who spent some part of their childhood in a foster home, group home, or institution, what are the processes by which these outcomes are produced? In addition to providing information regarding the outcomes of out-of-home care, the studies reviewed here provide some, albeit limited, ideas regarding those processes. The findings on this subject are summarized in the following chapter.

Chapter 10

Factors Associated with Outcomes of Out-of-Home Care

In Chapters 4 through 7, an attempt was made within each chapter that focused on a specific outcome to identify the specific process variables found to be associated with each of the outcomes. The process variables describe and differentiate the foster children and their experience in care, identifying which children are at greater risk of negative outcomes and how the out-of-home care experience itself may contribute to different outcomes. The function of this chapter is to look across the different outcomes in an attempt to provide an integrated perspective of the roles of specific process variables in determining outcomes.

While most of the criteria which have been used to rank studies are still of importance, the presence of comparative data, which was of central concern in assessing outcomes, is of less concern here. Our main interest in this chapter is in what differentiates the out-of-home care experience for its subjects. Comparisons with other groups are of less relevance.

Isolating effects is virtually impossible, given the high correlations between the process variables of interest (e.g., time spent in care, type of placement, age at placement, reason for placement). We search therefore for patterns rather than independent effects. Identification of these patterns can be an effective means to policy and program change that could lead to improved outcomes.

Type of Placement

As is true with all of the placement variables explored in this chapter, the findings regarding the association between type of placement and outcomes are not unidirectional. Nevertheless, positive outcomes appear to be more likely for children who have been placed in family foster care than in group or institutional care.

Subjects who had been in family foster care functioned better as adults than those who had spent all or part of their time in group settings: they completed more education [Festinger 1983]; they were less likely to have been arrested or convicted of a crime [Ferguson 1966; Festinger 1983; Jones & Moses 1984]; they were less likely to be dissatisfied with the amount of contact they had with their biological siblings at the time of the study [Festinger 1983]; they were less likely to have no close friends [Festinger 1983] and they had stronger informal support networks [Jones & Moses 1984]; they moved less often in adulthood; they were less likely to be living alone, to be single-parent heads of households, and to be divorced [Festinger 1983]; they were less likely to report alcohol or drug problems [Jones & Moses 1984]; they had a higher level of satisfaction with the amount of money they had for basics and with their financial situations; they had less of a sense that their incomes were below that of the average American; they had a stronger feeling that their financial situation had improved in the past few years and a higher level of optimism about future improvement in their situations; they assessed themselves and their lives more positively [Festinger 1983]; and they were more likely to be judged by interviewers as satisfied [Jones & Moses 1984].

The positive findings for family foster homes over group homes regarding drug and alcohol use and marriage were stronger for women. Women who had been placed in family foster homes, as opposed to those who had spent all or part of their time in group settings, were also less likely to have become pregnant for the first time while still in their teens and were less likely to be receiving public assistance [Festinger 1983].

Men who had been in foster homes were less likely than those who had been in group settings to have been arrested; and of the men who had been arrested, those from foster homes had been arrested less frequently than the others [Festinger 1983].

As stated above, there was some variation in the findings of the studies. Some outcomes favored group care over family foster care. Group settings seem to promote closer and more positive contacts with biological families. Subjects who were placed in group settings were more likely to marry and men were more likely to have children of their own [Jones & Moses 1984].

Overall, it appears that children who spend their time in care in family foster homes are functioning better as adults than those who spent at least part of their time in care in residential settings. A few of the authors note that this may be due, at least in part, to the nature of problems the children have when they enter care; children with more severe emotional, physical, or mental problems may be more likely to be placed in group settings than in foster homes, and they are more likely than the others to leave care with such problems. The results of these studies suggest that residential placements do not successfully ameliorate existing difficulties. If such amelioration is a goal of out-of-home care, then more effort must be made to develop family foster homes that can accommodate the special needs of these children.

Reason for Admission

A wide variety of data regarding the association between the reason for admission into out-of-home care and adult outcomes is presented in the studies included in this review. Because of this variety, as well as the differences across studies in the classifications of reasons for admission into care, conclusions are difficult to reach. However, some themes do begin to emerge. Before turning to differences, it should be noted that several studies found no relationship between reason for admission into care and the following outcome variables: IQ [Fox & Arcuri 1980]; overall picture of children's symptomatic behavior [Fanshel & Shinn 1978]; and the presence of serious health, social and emotional, and intellectual and learning problems [Festinger 1983].

Several studies [Kraus 1981; Fanshel & Shinn 1978; Jones & Moses 1984; Palmer 1976; Cook et al. 1991] attempted to identify those children who were placed in care because of their own behavior versus those placed for their own protection. One might expect that childhood behavioral problems so severe as to require out-of-home placement might result in more impaired adult functioning. However, in general, these studies did not find that this differentiation of reasons for placement was associated with later outcomes.

A more fruitful differentiation of the reason for placement focuses on the behavior of the parent(s). In general, placement because of neglect, abandonment, or physical abuse, compared to placement because of mental illness, death, imprisonment, or physical illness of the caretaker, was found to be associated with the following *negative* outcomes: more criminal behavior [Fanshel et al. 1990; Festinger 1983]; feeling less close to one or both parents [Festinger 1983]; poorer sense of well-being [Festinger 1983]; and lower educational achievement [Fanshel & Shinn 1978].

Age at Placement

Numerous studies investigated the relationship between the age of children at the time they entered care and their functioning as adults. The findings from these studies were highly variable and offered no convincing evidence that age at placement is a useful predictor of subsequent adult functioning. Most analyses failed to find significant relationships. For every finding that older children do better, there seems to be a contradictory finding.

One finding that does seem noteworthy comes from a single study. Festinger [1983] found that for the men who had been discharged from "group" settings, "older" age at the time of initial placement was associated with a stronger sense of well-being; however, for men discharged from "foster homes," "younger" age at placement was associated with a stronger sense of well-being. This finding, coupled with the general finding that negative outcomes are associated with group rather than family settings, suggests that early placement in the right setting can be beneficial, and that early placement in the wrong setting may be damaging.

Number of Placements

As is true with the other care variables examined in this chapter, the findings regarding the relationships between the number of placements a foster child has experienced and adult outcomes are not unanimous. However, this variable presents a clearer picture than the rest: fewer different placements while in care were associated with better adult functioning.

Living in fewer placements was found to be associated with better school achievement and more years of education [Palmer 1976; Zimmerman 1982; Cook et al. 1991]; increased contacts with and feelings of closeness to foster families after discharge [Festinger 1983]; less criminal activity [Zimmerman 1982]; more informal social supports [Jones & Moses 1984]; increased life satisfaction [Jones & Moses 1984; Triseliotis & Russell 1984]; greater housing stability [Meier 1965]; self-support [Zimmerman 1982]; increased ability to access health care; better chance to avoid early parenthood and being a cost to the community [Cook et al. 1991]; and better care for one's own children [Zimmerman 1982].

It should be noted that analyses can be found for almost all of the above outcome variables which yielded no significant relationship with number of placements. The preponderance of evidence, however, points to higher numbers of placements being associated with less successful outcomes.

Fanshel et al. [1990], as a result of their more recent study of former residents of the Casey Family Program, hypothesized a sequence of variables in a causal chain that ultimately determines the adult condition of people who had been in care when they were children. The number of living arrangements in which the children had resided entering the Casey program was the first link in this chain; those foster children who had experienced multiple placements prior to their admission into the program seemed destined to poorer outcomes than those with fewer placements.

Time in Care

As long as they don't go from home to home

While one study found longer time in care associated with greater likelihood of early parenthood and becoming a cost to the community [Cook et al. 1991], considerable evidence supports the benefits of being in care for longer periods of time. Longer time in placement was found to be associated with a higher degree of life satisfaction [Jones & Moses 1984], improved adult functioning [Zimmerman 1982], better psychological functioning [Palmer 1976; Fanshel & Shinn 1978; Frost & Jurich 1983], and less criminal activity [Kraus 1981; Zimmerman 1982].

strongly agree

Several studies provide insights into how or under what conditions time is associated with positive outcomes. Benefits are maximized when the long-term placement is in a normal, stable, foster family setting [Zimmerman 1982]. Under these conditions, the child develops greater emotional ties and identification with the foster family rather than the biological family, maintains contact with the foster family, and receives their support in adulthood [Festinger 1983; Jones & Moses 1984].

Stability of the out-of-home care placement and adequacy of the home to which a child is returned are factors which seem to have some bearing on the effects of length of time in care. If children are returned to homes in which their needs are not sufficiently met, they may be harmed more in the long run than they would have been had they remained in out-of-home care. But long-term care may be beneficial only if the child is able to spend most of this time in a single, stable placement.

Age at Discharge

Very few findings are reported that pertain to the relationship between the age at which a child is discharged from care and adult outcome variables. While not identical, age at discharge is highly correlated with time in care. Not surprisingly, the studies that addressed this relationship found that older age at discharge was positively associated with adequate functioning as an adult [Zimmerman 1982], with not having been convicted of a crime [Zimmerman 1982], and with feeling more satisfaction with life as an adult [Jones & Moses 1984].

Disposition

Most of the authors who explored the relationship between adult functioning and the nature of the foster child's disposition from care studied the differences between children who were returned to their own homes and those who remained in some form of care until they aged out. A greater number of the study findings associated negative outcomes with returning home rather than remaining in care [Fanshel & Shinn 1978; Ferguson 1966; Zimmerman 1982]. In particular, those returned home seemed more likely to engage in criminal activity.

Consistent with the findings reported above regarding the "time in care" variable, subjects returning home were found to have stronger ties to their biological family than to the foster family.

Caseworker Activity

Only four studies reported associations between outcomes and the nature of the social services provided to the child. Cook et al. [1991] report that study youths who received independent living skills training exhibited better outcomes with respect to eight measures including: ability to maintain a job for at least one year, ability to access health care, not being a cost to the community, completing high school, having a social network, overall satisfaction with life, and a composite outcome measure. However, this impact is dependent upon matching of specific skill training and desired outcomes (i.e., health skills training showed effects on obtaining health care, and the receipt of employment skills training resulted in being less of a cost to the community).

Only one additional study, Fanshel and Shinn [1978], is of reasonable quality and makes any serious attempt to explore this topic, but it does not follow subjects into adulthood.

In Fanshel and Shinn, the provision of services was variously conceptualized and operationalized to include the level of education of the worker, number of workers, skill of the worker, experience of the worker, type of placement agency (voluntary v. public; religious v. secular), and amount of casework activity. The lack of substantial and consistent findings on any one of these variables makes it impossible to draw even tentative conclusions.

Contact and Closeness with Biological and Foster Families

Eight investigations included data which were related to the impact of family relationships upon various outcomes. As with many of the other variables, the outcomes are mixed, making it difficult to draw conclusions. The summary of findings begins with a description of the impact of the amount of contact the children in care had with their biological families during care and then examines closeness with biological and foster families. A few findings pertain to the relationship between these two types of families.

Several studies indicated that there was a positive relationship between a variety of outcomes and the amount of contact the foster children had with members of their biological family while in placement. As one might expect, greater contact with the biological family while the child was in placement was found to be associated with greater feelings of closeness and identification with the biological family [Festinger 1983; Zimmerman 1982]. Greater contact also appears to be associated with lower levels of serious problems at discharge [Fanshel & Shinn 1978]. However, both positive and negative associations were found between contact with the biological family during placement and adult functioning [Festinger 1983; Triseliotis & Russell 1984; Zimmerman 1982].

Findings regarding feelings of closeness or identification with the biological family also ranged from positive to negative but, more often than not, these feelings were not associated with outcomes achieved as adults [Festinger 1983; Palmer 1976]. On the other hand, associations between outcome variables and the subjects' relationships with their foster caregivers generally were either positive or neutral in their effects on adult functioning. Increased closeness and identification with the foster parents during care was found to be related to good academic and social progress while in care [Palmer 1976]; the absence of task, emotional, or behavioral problems at the end of care [Palmer 1976]; and greater sense of well-being and life satisfaction as adults [Festinger 1983; Jones & Moses 1984; Zimmerman 1982].

Summary

It is obvious that one must exercise extreme care in making any causal interpretations of the findings presented here. The likelihood of spurious correlation is high. On the other hand, these associations point to specific areas where further exploration might be fruitful.

Most of the findings are consistent with practice and policy knowledge supporting the use of foster family placement over group or institutional placement and stressing the need for stability in placement. Other findings, however, strongly contradict current thinking in the out-of-home care field—that long-term foster care is harmful for the child. Several studies suggest that a stable long-term placement in a family foster home where the child is able to develop a strong identification with the foster family can actually benefit the individual as an adult.

Chapter 11

Next Steps

Having reviewed what we know about the adult outcomes of those formerly in care as children and about the factors associated with those outcomes, we are now ready to recommend the next steps in a research agenda designed to provide more definitive answers and to track progress in this area. Additional efforts to determine the long-term outcomes of out-of-home care are needed for several reasons. First, out-of-home care is, and will likely continue to be, a major service response for some children when their family life becomes untenable. As a service response, long-term out-of-home care should not be viewed as a failure. Like Jim Casey and Joseph Reid, the founders of the Casey Family Program, we believe that quality long-term out-of-home care will continue to be the *most desirable solution* to the needs of a sizable number of children and their families. As shown in the numerous studies reviewed in this book, an extended stay in out-of-home care as a child does not necessarily condemn the individual to an unhappy and unproductive adult life and may indeed lead to more beneficial outcomes than would reunification with parents. Given an ongoing need and positive rationale for the service, we must seek to optimize the chances for positive outcomes for out-of-home care.

Second, the failure to achieve positive adult outcomes for a significant portion of subjects who were once in care creates additional demands for more serious study of this area. While definitive conclusions cannot be drawn from the review of studies presented in this book, we believe that these studies do offer convincing evidence that children in care are at high risk of "rotten" outcomes as adults. These outcomes are not simply a slightly diminished functioning or a failure to reach full potential, but may involve a failure to meet minimal levels of self-sufficiency (homelessness, welfare dependency, etc.) and acceptable behaviors (criminal activity, substance abuse, etc.). A problem of this magnitude deserves additional attention. Perhaps transitional service programs for the adolescent out-of-home care population can be reframed to provide support for those at risk of these "rotten" adult outcomes rather than focus on the failure to preserve the family. Regardless of the strategy employed to ameliorate the risk, we believe the need is urgent.

Finally, although it is customary for research reviews to end with a call for more research, we believe that a particularly strong case can be made for research on the long-term effects of out-of-home care. To some, the fact that 29 separate studies were identified covering more than 30 years might appear impressive. We would argue that this is a meager corpus, given the length of time out-of-home care has been used and the high emotional and financial costs involved in the delivery of this service. In contrast, a recent metaanalysis found the effects of anxiety on sport performance found 50 studies published between 1970 and 1988 [Kleine 1990], another recent metaanalysis found 46 studies of intervention programs for juvenile delinquents [Izzo & Ross 1990].

In judging the research available on the long-term effects of out-of-home care, one must also take into consideration its quality. Overall, we find the quality to be poor. Most of the research designs simply do not provide an opportunity for adequately answering the questions framed in Chapter 3 involving the long-term outcomes of out-of-home care. The remainder of this chapter focuses on a critique of the research methodologies and provides specific recommendations for future research.

Direct Out-of-Home Care Studies

This review focused on studies of the lives of subjects who had left out-of-home care; that is, the studies looked directly at the outcomes of such care. These 29 studies are listed in Appendix A. These "direct" studies are to be distinguished from studies which, while reporting outcomes for subjects formerly in care, have as their primary focus the examination of some problem area or population. The latter "outcome studies" are exemplified by the six studies of homeless populations, which are listed in Appendix C and are discussed further in the following section.

With respect to the direct studies of the effects of out-of-home care, the methodological critique in Chapter 3 identified five criteria: use of a control group, age of subjects when the study took place, sample size, dropout rate, and study date. Three of these attributes are fairly obvious and require little further comment. In general, the more recently the study was conducted, the older the subjects, and the larger the sample, the more confidence we are able to have in the findings.

Sampling bias was a major concern in the majority of the direct studies. This is in large part a function of the designs used. Most studies employed retrospective designs, for which low response rate is an inherent problem. Of the retrospective studies, two [Kraus 1981; Dumaret 1985] achieved high response rates by utilizing record checks with relatively stable populations. Dumaret's study also involved a short period since care, as did Allerhand et al.'s [1966] study, which had a nonresponse rate of only 4%. The 16 remaining retrospective studies for which rates could be calculated had nonresponse rates ranging from 20% to 78%. In contrast, in the studies that used prospective designs the attrition rates ranged from 1% to 21% [McCord et al. 1960; Ferguson 1966; Quinton et al. 1986].

The potential bias resulting from the high dropout rates in the retrospective studies makes them of little practical use. We believe that there is little to be gained from further retrospective studies unless steps can be taken to guarantee lower dropout rates than those found here. It is interesting to note that dropout rates associated with earlier studies (pre-1980) appear to be lower than those associated with the set of retrospective studies undertaken in the 1980s. The earlier studies also typically involved smaller samples. It is possible that these early studies devoted more resources to tracking down a smaller study group, or perhaps, as the population has become more transient, tracking has become more difficult.

A second criterion—whether or not the study provided a direct comparison group—not only is critical to the internal validity of the studies but also determines how the study findings can be used. In ranking studies with regard to this criterion, we differentiated three types: (1) single-sample studies with no normative data; (2) single-sample studies with normative data; and (3) multisample comparison-group studies.

Single-sample studies, which overcome attrition problems (e.g., Allerhand et al. [1966]) can provide useful descriptive information. Proper planning and analysis of data from these studies can provide considerable insight into the causes of variations in outcomes *within* the population in out-of-home care. These studies are most useful in addressing the process questions summarized in the preceding chapter.

The introduction of normative data in single-sample studies (by use of standardized tests or results from other population surveys) is an attempt to ascertain the actual impact of the out-of-home care experience on those placed in care. Such data, which we have ourselves added in our description of certain study findings, can be useful for providing a broad context for interpreting outcome findings. For example, it is difficult to know what to make of marriage rates for subjects formerly in out-of-home care without knowing what the rate is for the general population. If the rates for the two are the same, we can conclude that this is not an area of concern with regard to the adult outcomes for children formerly in care. If the rates differ, however, interpretation is extremely difficult owing to the large number of alternative explanations (e.g., poverty, race, geographic representation). Attempts at statistical control or matching to achieve equivalency in comparison data of this type are generally not convincing and too susceptible to manipulation and interpretation by the researcher or reader.

Chapters 4 through 7 presented a synthesis of findings on various adult outcomes. In these chapters, we have relegated the studies that do not provide a direct comparison group to a lesser role in describing the outcomes achieved. Although all the reviewed studies present findings on outcomes, this information is purely descriptive unless the study can additionally answer the question, "Compared to what?"

Eight of the 29 reviewed studies can be described as multisample comparison-group studies because they include a direct comparison group in the study design. Although most of the reviewed studies (65%) were done in the United States, five of the eight studies that include comparison groups were conducted in other countries. Thus, the potential for quasiexperimental designs exists, but this potential has not been fully exploited in past research, particularly in the United States.

Selection of a comparison group is critical in that it largely determines the conclusions that can be drawn from differential outcomes. The eight studies that include comparison groups have employed a variety of strategies in selecting the subjects for the comparison group. Several studies employed matching techniques. Heston et al. [1966] used a two-factor design that looked at the effects of placement and psychiatric history of the mother. Frommer and O'Shea [1973a; 1973b] were interested in identifying factors that might be predictive of mothers having problems raising their children. Hypothesizing that the mother's out-of-home placement might be one such factor, the researchers identified users of antenatal clinics in London who had experienced such separations, and chose controls from those reporting no separation. Controls were matched with the separated subjects by age, social class, and expected date of delivery. Quinton et al. [1986] were also interested in determining whether there is a continuity between adverse experiences in childhood and poor parenting behavior in adult life. Their study compared women who had been residents of one of two children's homes with subjects matched for age and living in the same general area of the inner city as children but never admitted into care.

Other studies have employed more naturally occurring control groups without matching. Wolkind's [1977a; 1977b] research was similar to Frommer and O'Shea's in that it examined factors affecting the future maternal role of first-time pregnant women. Wolkind's study, however, did not match subjects but simply noted whether any of the women had been in placement as children. Only 7% had experienced placement, but the large sample ($N = 534$) yielded sufficient numbers for comparison purposes. Robins [1966] simply focused on all former patients of a child guidance clinic and noted whether they had been in placement.

When confronted with a confirmed situation of abuse or neglect, the social service system and family are faced with basically three alternatives: long-term placement (group or family foster care), adoption, or maintaining the child in the family of origin. Only three studies, however, have patterned their research designs to directly model this decision point. Triseliotis and Russell [1984] compared adoptees with long-term residents in institutions, all of whom were from highly disadvantaged backgrounds. Comparisons from an earlier sample of family foster care subjects were also made

[Triseliotis 1980]. Runyan and Gould [1985], in the only U.S. study of this type, compared children placed in family foster care for a minimum of three years with matched maltreated children who were provided services in their own homes. Dumaret's [1985] study provides the most complete group design, comparing adoptees, children in out-of-home care, and children who remained in their own homes. All of the children were from disadvantaged backgrounds and had been placed at one time with "a view to adoption."

By providing a direct basis for comparison of the outcomes achieved by subjects who were once in care, these eight studies are in the best position to assess the long-term impact of out-of-home care. They further demonstrate that rigorous designs can be successfully used in conducting research on out-of-home care outcomes. The dearth of such research, particularly in this country, attests to the lack of attention that this question has received.

The current lack of uniformity in the treatment of abuse and neglect in this country, while deplorable from a policy and practice perspective, does provide a rich opportunity for the use of "natural experiments." Studies could be designed to take advantage of existing variation across geographic areas in the intervention and placement practices of agencies. In effect, we have an experimental opportunity when children experiencing the same basic conditions in basically identical family situations may be placed in out-of-home care or adoptive homes or left in their own homes, depending merely on where they live. The impact of this variation in placement interventions should be systematically investigated, so that we can begin to provide uniform treatment based on evidence of the efficacy of our interventions.

While advocating the increased use of quasiexperimental designs that employ naturally occurring comparison groups (adoptees, in-home, and out-of-home care subjects), we would also like to raise the possibility of employing even more rigorous research designs, which include random assignment.

Although one may initially question the feasibility—even the ethics—of randomly assigning abused or neglected children to alternative placement settings, available evidence suggests that the decisions currently being made approximate a random process. The idiosyncratic nature of placement decisions and resulting inequalities in treatment of children and families are widely discussed and documented in the literature [Lindsey 1991; Mech 1970; Packman et al. 1986; Fanshel & Shinn 1978; Costin et al. 1991]. Several recent evaluations of family preservation services have raised doubts about our ability to operationalize the concept of "imminent risk of placement" and ultimately to prevent placement [Nelson 1990]. If professionals and researchers in the field cannot identify children who are at risk of placement, and if there is no evidence that out-of-home placement is a function of the child's and family's needs, can a strong argument be made against random assignment?

Clearly, no child who is at risk of harm should have that risk increased to satisfy a research agenda. Yet, available data suggest that the majority of children identified as being in need of placement do not get placed, regardless of the type of intervention provided by the protective service agency or family preservation program [Nelson 1990]. Barth and Berry [1987] have argued that children who remain in their own homes may be more poorly served than children who are placed in out-of-home care or adopted. Consistent with this perspective, we are seeing increasing numbers of children returned home only to then return to the out-of-home care system [Rzepnicki 1987]. Our reading of this situation is that we simply do not know the effects of our actions on the children in need of services. Isn't it time to embark on a line of research and service that will better inform our efforts?

The above discussion of the use of random assignment has focused on comparisons of long-term out-of-home care versus in-home alternatives. We believe that fairly strong evidence exists of the benefits of adoption for this population of children. Adoptive placements appear stable and discharge outcomes are generally positive [McDonald et al. 1989; Barth & Berry 1988]. The available evidence from the relatively longer-term studies reviewed here, while meager, also suggests that these subjects fare well as adults. Given these results, adoption, when available as an option, should generally be pursued rather than long-term out-of-home care. It is possible, however, that long-term care may be more desirable than adoption for special subpopulations of children in care. For example, Festinger [1983] found that having a relative for a foster parent is better than being adopted by an unrelated family. It would be important to find out what the long-term outcomes of out-of-home care placements with relatives are, compared to adoption.

Indirect Outcome Studies

In the presentation in Chapter 4 of self-sufficiency outcomes achieved by adults once in care as children, we included findings from several studies of the homeless. These studies did not have as their primary purpose the investigation of long-term outcomes of out-of-home care, but rather were focused on the problem of homelessness itself. The studies included information about out-of-home placement of the subjects who were homeless as possible predictors or risk factors which might explain the phenomenon of homelessness. Prior placement was but one such predictor and, as such, may not receive much attention in the reported findings of these studies. We were aware of these findings because two of us have conducted extensive studies in this area and also share an interest in and knowledge of the child welfare field. Similar findings might be found with respect to any of the other outcome areas addressed in this review (e.g., unemployment, criminal behavior, chemical dependency, marriage, parenting and social relationships, and mental and physical health). A literature search of each of these areas, however, would be like looking for a needle in a haystack, since the focus was not specifically on the impact of out-of-home placement and many of the studies undoubtedly ignored this aspect altogether.

We wish to draw attention to the potential role of out-of-home placement as a predictor of various adult functioning outcomes. We suggest that it be included in future outcome-oriented studies where the focus may not necessarily be on the impact of out-of-home placement.

Similarly, large, multipurpose, general population surveys should recognize the potential importance of out-of-home placement as a variable of interest to researchers who might use these data. This potential is demonstrated in the most recent study reviewed in this book, where Cook [1992] was able to identify a sample of 107 children formerly in care in the 1988 National Survey of Families and Households. Placement as a child was found to be a highly predictive independent variable in this study of adult well-being.

Interpretation of findings from outcome-oriented studies that include information about the placement status of their subjects as children is relatively straightforward. Furthermore, such studies may provide rich information on the adult lives of subjects formerly in care. The critical question, from the perspective of this review, is whether the subjects formerly in care are overrepresented in the particular problem population under consideration. For example, the homeless studies reviewed found 15% to 35% of their subjects had been in out-of-home placement as children. Is this high or low? What is needed is an estimate of the percentage of children formerly in care in the adult population. Gershenson [1993], currently with the Center for the Study of Social Policy, and longtime director of research for the Children's Bureau at the U.S. Department of Health and Human Services, estimates that approximately four million Americans (1% to 2%) have been in care at least once. This percentage would increase to about 4% if one includes mental health and juvenile justice admissions. These numbers provide a clear picture of the dramatically higher risk of homelessness subjects formerly in care face as adults.

Summary

The majority of studies that have directly considered the adult experience of subjects once in care have employed retrospective, single-group designs. These studies have the potential to describe this experience and to identify important predictors of variations in outcomes for the subjects. This information also has important implications for the field, which should strive to achieve the most positive outcomes for all children in care. Methodological flaws, however, particularly attrition, have limited the utility of these studies. In addition, these studies cannot ultimately tell us if the lives of subjects formerly in care are enhanced or further impaired by their experience in care.

Studies of out-of-home care that provide a direct comparison group offer the best alternative for addressing gaps in our knowledge about the adult functioning of subjects formerly in care. A handful of such studies have been done, proving that it is feasible. The majority of these studies have been conducted outside the United States, suggesting that this question has not yet received the attention that it deserves in this country. In pursuing additional studies of this type, researchers should look to the quasiexperimental designs employed in the studies described here, but they should also consider more rigorous designs that include random assignment. We believe that for a significant number of children, the decision to place them in out-of-home care or leave them in their parents' home is currently arbitrary, and the consequences of this decision are largely unknown. We owe it to these children and to the thousands of children who will be in similar situations to search for the answers now.

Appendixes

Appendix A

Studies of Outcomes of Out-of-Home Care (Table)

STUDY	TYPE OF STUDY	CHARACTERISTICS OF SAMPLE
McCord, J., McCord, W., & Thurber, E. (1960). The Effects of Foster Home Placement in the Prevention of Adult Antisocial Behavior. *Social Service Review, 34,* 415–419.	Prospective, with comparison group	$N = 38$ (19 in out-of-home) Ages: early 30s Selection criteria: Follow-up of an earlier delinquency prevention study in Massachusetts. Of 24 children removed from their homes as young adolescents, data were available on 19, who became subjects. Matched comparison group was drawn from remaining sample ($N = 236$).
Maas, H. S. (1963). The Young Adult of Former Foster Children. *Child Welfare, 44,* 196–206.	Retrospective, no comparison group	$N = 20$ Ages: 19–26 Selection criteria: Placed for at least 1 year as preschool children for their safety by parents in British wartime residential nurseries; average stay over 3 years.
Meier, E. G. (1965). Current Circumstances of Former Foster Children. *Child Welfare, 44,* 196–206.	Retrospective, no comparison group	$N = 66$ Ages: 28–32 Selection criteria: Adults who as children had experienced 5 or more years of family foster care in Minnesota, who had not been returned to their own families during their childhoods, and who were discharged from guardianship between 7/1/48 and 12/31/49. Attempted to use all eligible males and a random sample of eligible females.

Note: All Ns are final sample sizes, after attrition had taken place

Outcomes Studied	Data Collection	Dropout Rate
Criminal behavior, alcoholism, mental health.	Observation of children and families.	21%
Living arrangements, employment, leisure-time interests, education, and family life, Thematic Apperception Test.	All subjects interviewed; 14 observed with families; parents of 18 interviewed; records of collateral agencies.	78% (Appears that first 20 successful contacts were used)
Social effectiveness and sense of well-being; includes family life, living arrangements, economic-employment history, community involvement.	Interviews and questionnaires; phone calls or letters from those who refused to participate in full study.	20%

STUDY	TYPE OF STUDY	CHARACTERISTICS OF SAMPLE
Allerhand, M. E., Weber, R. E., & Haug, M. (1966). *Adaptation and adaptability: The Bellefaire follow-up study.* New York: Child Welfare League of America.	Retrospective, no comparison group	N = 50 Ages: 18 average Selection criteria: All boys discharged from Bellefaire in Cleveland, OH, between 1/58 and 6/61 who were in care at least 6 months.
Ferguson, T. (1966). *Children in care—and after.* London: Oxford University Press.	Prospective, no comparison group; normative data provided	N = 203 Ages: 18–20 Selection criteria: Youth in care of the Children's Department of Glasgow, Scotland, until age 18; left care between 1961 and 1963.
Heston, L. L., Denney, D. D., & Pauly, I. B. (1966). The Adult Adjustment of Persons Institutionalized as Children. *British Journal of Psychiatry, 112,* 1103–1110.	Retrospective, with comparison group	N = 97 (47 in placement) Ages: 21–50 Selection criteria: Subjects placed in foundling homes in Oregon; 25 born to schizophrenic mothers in state psychiatric hospitals; average stay over 2 years.
Robins, L. N. (1966). *Deviant children grown up: A sociological and psychiatric study of sociopathic personality.* Baltimore: Williams and Wilkins.	Retrospective, with comparison group	N = 491 (401 in placement) Ages: 27–53 Selection criteria: 524 former child guidance clinic patients, 16% whom had lived in foster homes and 16% in orphanages for 6 months or more prior to referral to the clinic.

Note: All Ns are final sample sizes, after attrition had taken place.

Outcomes Studied	Data Collection	Dropout Rate
Adaptability (intrapsychic balance and total role fulfillment) and adaptation (interpersonal and cultural role fulfillment).	Agency records; interviews with subjects, their parents, and psychotherapist if currently in treatment. Interviews held 1 to 2 years after discharge: between 1959 and 1963.	4%
Educational achievement, health, employment-economic history, criminal behavior, family life and relationships, recreation.	Agency records, school teachers' reports, interviews with subjects every 6 months for 2 years after discharge from care. Data collected 1961–65.	1%
MMPI scores, socioeconomic status, psychosocial disability, psychiatric diagnosis.	Interviews, record reviews.	27%
School problems and achievement, marital history, adult relationships, military service, job history, history of arrests and imprisonments, financial dependency, geographic moves, history of deviant behavior, physical and psychiatric diseases, alcohol and drug use, intellectual level, cooperativeness, willingness to talk, frankness, and mood.	Interviews.	21%

Study	Type of Study	Characteristics of Sample
Maas, H. S. (1969). Children in long term foster care. *Child Welfare, 48,* 321–333, 347.	Retrospective, no comparison group	$N = 422$ Ages: N/A Selection criteria: Children studied by Maas and Engler in the late 1950s; all had been in foster care for at least 3 months in 1 of 9 U. S. counties as of 4/1/57. Eight of the nine original counties participated in this study.
Frommer, E. A., & O'Shea, G. (1973a). Antenatal identification of women liable to have problems in managing their infants. *British Journal of Psychiatry, 123,* 149–156. (1973b). The importance of childhood experience in relation to problems of marriage and family building. *British Journal of Psychiatry, 1,* 123, 157–160.	Retrospective, with comparison group; prospective, with comparison group	$N = 89$ (45 "separated" at time 1) Age: Not reported Selection criteria: Stratified sample of all married British-born first-time pregnant women attending antenatal clinics in London, half of whom had experienced early separation (before age 11) from their biological families.
Palmer, S. E. (1976). *Children in long term care: Their experience and progress.* Canada: Family and Children's Services of London and Middlesex.	Retrospective, no comparison; limited normative data	$N = 200$ Ages: 18–21 Selection criteria: Children once in the care of two Children's Aid Society agencies in Toronto, Canada, and the C.A.S. in London, England. They were at least three years old when they left their families; minimum of 5 years in care ending when they reached majority (or up to age 21 if still in school); did not have physical or mental condition severe enough to keep them from leading a normal life; not from a distinct cultural background.

Note: All Ns are final sample sizes, after attrition had taken place.

Outcomes Studied	Data Collection	Dropout Rate
Disposition from care and length of time in care.	Original study: agency records; collected data in 1957 and 1958. This study: agency staff completed questionnaires in 1967.	23%
Feelings toward the child and husband, physical and mental health, expected financial impact of having a baby, behavior of the infant.	Interview and observation.	28% dropout at time 1; 32% at time 2
Social progress (improvement in behavior, performance, and emotional problems and academic progress).	Agency records. Date of data collection not given; probably early 1970s.	46%

STUDY	TYPE OF STUDY	CHARACTERISTICS OF SAMPLE
Wolkind, S. N. (1977a). A child's relationship after admission to residential care. *Child Care, Health, and Development, 3,* 357–362. (1977b). Women who have been 'In care'—psychological and social status during pregnancy." *Journal of Child Psychology and Psychiatry, 18,* 179–182.	Retrospective, with comparison	$N = 534$ (36 placed in care) Age: Not reported Selection criteria: First-time pregnant women attending obstetric clinic in London; separated from their families at least 3 months before age 16.
Fanshel, D., & Shinn, E. B. (1978). *Children in foster care: A longitudinal investigation.* New York: Columbia University.	Retrospective, no comparison group	$N = 624$ Ages: 5–17 Selection criteria: Entered New York City's foster care system in 1966 and were in care at least 90 days; newborn to 12 years of age at entry; first entry into care. Used an age and gender quota system.
Harari, T. (1980). *Teenagers exiting from family foster care: A retrospective look* (Ph.D. dissertation, University of California, Berkeley).	Retrospective, no comparison group	$N = 34$ Age: 17–23 (19.8 average) Selection criteria: Turned 18 by 2/78; had left care as adolescents between 1/74 and 6/78; had been in care a minimum of 1.5 years, not diagnosed as mentally retarded; still living in northern California.
Fox, M., & Arcuri, K. (1980). Cognitive and academic functioning in foster children. *Child Welfare, 59,* 491–496.	Retrospective, no comparison group but standardized tests used	$N = 163$ Ages: 5–18 Selection criteria: All children in care of Children's Aid Society of Pennsylvania in 1978.

Note: All Ns are final sample sizes, after attrition had taken place.

Outcomes Studied	Data Collection	Dropout Rate
History of housing or social problems; presence of psychiatric and chronic physical disorders.	Interviews.	5%
Status changes experienced by children; changes in their personal and social adjustment.	IQ and projective tests, behavioral ratings and developmental profiles, teacher assessments, and reports from parents, subjects, caseworkers. Data collected 1966–1971. (Not all data were collected for all subjects.)	Potential sample = ? Final sample = 624
"Current life experience;" interpersonal affect and self-esteem scales from Jackson personality inventory.	Interviews.	60%
Cognitive and academic skills; grade level.	Standardized tests including Wechsler Intelligence Tests and Wide Range Achievement Test.	0% for intelligence tests; 14% for WRAT-Reading; 65% for WRAT-Arithmetic

Study	Type of Study	Characteristics of Sample
Triseliotis, J. (1980). Growing up in foster care and after. In J. Triseliotis, ed., *New developments in foster care and adoption*. London: Routledge & Kegan Paul.	Retrospective, no comparison group	$N = 40$ Ages: 20–21 Selection criteria: Scottish study of subjects born in 1956 and 1957 who had spent 7 to 15 years in a single foster home before age 16.
Kraus, J. (1981). Foster children grown up: Parameters of care and adult delinquency. *Children and Youth Services Review, 3*, 99–114.	Retrospective, no comparison group	$N = 491$ Ages: 27–28 Selection criteria: All former wards of the state of New South Wales, Australia, born 1951 and 1952, and discharged at age 18 into situations other than the care of their family or relatives; averaged 9.3 years in care.
Zimmerman, R. B. (1982). *Foster care in retrospect. Tulane Studies in Social Welfare, 14*.	Retrospective, no comparison group; limited normative data	$N = 61$ Ages: 19–29 Selection criteria: Former foster children in New Orleans who entered care between 1951 and 1969, had been in a foster home for at least a year, and had not been adopted; only one child from any one family.

Note: All Ns are final sample sizes, after attrition had taken place.

Outcomes Studied	Data Collection	Dropout Rate
Educational achievement, employment history, family life, living arrangements, contact with foster family, coping ability, sense of well-being, criminal behavior, and perceptions of social workers.	Interviews with former foster children and their foster parents: conducted in 1976 and 1977.	32%
Criminal activity.	Criminal and welfare records.	None
Educational achievement, financial status, life satisfaction, family life and relationships, social support, views regarding fostering experience, employment, health, history of mental illness or antisocial behavior.	Interviews. March–April, 1980.	64%

STUDY	TYPE OF STUDY	CHARACTERISTICS OF SAMPLE
Festinger, T. (1983). *No one ever asked us: A postscript to foster care.* New York: Columbia University Press.	Retrospective, no comparison group; normative data provided	N = 277 Ages: 22–26 Selection criteria: Young adults who had been discharged from out-of-home care in the New York metropolitan area in 1975, who had been in care continuously for at least the preceding 5 years, and 18 to 21 years old at discharge.
Frost, S., & Jurich, A. P. (1983). Follow–up study of children residing in the Villages (unpublished report). *The Villages,* Topeka, KS.	Retrospective, no comparison group	N = 95 Ages: N/A Selection criteria: Former foster children who had lived in group care at the Villages in Topeka, Kansas, for at least 6 months.
Jones, M. A., & Moses, B. (1984). *West Virginia's former foster children: Their experiences in care and their lives as young adults.* New York: Child Welfare League of America.	Retrospective, no comparison group; limited normative data	N = 328 Ages: 19–28 Selection criteria: Young adults who had received foster care in West Virginia for at least 1 year after 10/1/77 but before 1/1/84 and who were at least 19 years of age on 1/1/84.
Rest, E. R., & Watson, K. W. (1984). Growing up in foster care. *Child Welfare, 63,* 291–306.	Retrospective, no comparison group	N = 13 Ages: 19–31 Selection criteria: Former foster children once in the care of Chicago Child Care Society; entered care at age 6 or younger and reached maturity within the agency's program; discharged as independent functioning adults between 1966 and 1981.

Note: All Ns are final sample sizes, after attrition had taken place.

OUTCOMES STUDIED	DATA COLLECTION	DROPOUT RATE
Well-being, family life and relationships, personal problems, social support, educational achievement, employment, finances, health, drug/alcohol use, criminal behavior, use of formal help-providers, perceptions of fostering experience.	In-person and phone interviews, questionnaires. Data collected between 5/79 and 4/80.	54%
Educational achievement, employment, social support, legal history, financial status, overall functioning level, satisfaction with care.	Personal and telephone interviews, questionnaires: conducted in 1982 and 1983.	46%
Living arrangements, employment and finances, social support, family life and relationships, evaluation of care received, education, health, legal history, alcohol/drug use, life satisfaction.	Personal and telephone interviews, questionnaires. Data collected in 1984.	48%
Perceptions of experience of care and the impact of this on current life, employment, family life and relationships, self-concept.	Interviews: 1981.	Not reported

STUDY	TYPE OF STUDY	CHARACTERISTICS OF SAMPLE
Triseliotis, J., & Russell, J. (1984). *Hard to place: The outcome of adoption and residential care.* London: Heinemann.	Retrospective, with comparison group	$N = 84$ (40 in residential care, 44 adoptees) Ages: mean of 24 for adoptees and 22.8 for residential care. Selection criteria: Children who had been in the care of public child welfare agencies and 1 private placement agency in Scotland, who had either been adopted or else placed in a residential facility, and who were in their 20s at the time of the study. All were from very disadvantaged backgrounds. Adoptees: 2–10 years old at the time placed in adoptive homes. Foster children: placed in 1 or more residential establishments by age 10 and stayed there until at least 16.
Dumaret, A. 1985. IQ, scholastic performance, and behaviors of sibs raised in contrasting environments. *Journal of Child Psychology and Psychiatry and Allied Disciplines, 26,* 553–580.	Retrospective, with comparison groups	$N = 104$ (35 adoptees, 48 own home, 21 foster care) Ages: N/A Selection criteria: French study of the offspring of 28 mothers from a disadvantaged background who had abandoned their children with "a view to adoption."
Runyan, D. K., & Gould, C. (1985). Foster care for child maltreatment: impact on delinquent behavior. *Pediatrics, 75,* 562–568.	Retrospective, with comparison group	$N = 114$ foster children $= 106$ comparison Ages: average of 14 Selection criteria: Maltreated children in 6 central North Carolina counties who had been in family foster care a minimum of 3 years. Controls were matched to maltreated children who were provided services in their own homes.

Note: All Ns are final sample sizes, after attrition had taken place.

OUTCOMES STUDIED	DATA COLLECTION	DROPOUT RATE
Employment, living arrangements, mental health problems, educational achievement, financial status, family life and relationships, health, criminal behavior, alcohol use, social support, coping capability, life satisfaction. Contrasts with biological families.	Agency records; interviews and questionnaires, 1978–80.	47%
IQ, school performance and behavior, job history and status (for older subjects).	Tests of subjects (in school), questionnaire to teachers, records. Most of testing done in schools. Neither mothers nor children knew they were being studied. Unclear how the job history data were collected (probably record reviews).	None
Juvenile delinquency.	Abstracting of cumulative files maintained by social service agency, juvenile courts, and schools.	?

Study	**Type of Study**	**Characteristics of Sample**
Quinton, D., Rutter, M., & Liddle, C. (1986). Institutional rearing, parenting difficulties, and marital support. In S. Chess & A. Thomas (Eds.), *Annual progress in child psychiatry and child development, 1985.* New York: Brunner/Mazel.	Prospective, with comparison group	N = 81 (formerly in care group) = 41 (control) Ages: 21–27 Selection criteria: Two groups of British women first studied as children in the mid-1960s. First group were girls who had been residents in one of two children's homes. Comparison group were same age as formerly in care group, never had been in care, lived with families in same geographic area and had had school behavior assessed at same age with same questionnaire.
Fanshel, D., Finch, S. J., & Grundy, J. F. (1990). *Foster children in life course perspective.* New York: Columbia University Press.	Retrospective, no comparison	N = 106 106 were interviewed Ages: Early 20s to mid 30s; average = 24 Selection criteria: All former foster children who had been in placement with the Casey Family Program between 1966 and 1984 and had been discharged by 12/31/84. Included divisions in Washington, Idaho, Montana, California, and Oregon.

Note: All Ns are final sample sizes, after attrition had taken place.

OUTCOMES STUDIED	DATA COLLECTION	
Overall style of parenting, effectiveness and consistency of control, parental sensitivity to the child's needs, expressed warmth toward and criticism of the child.	Interviews with women and spouses, and direct observation of mother-child interactions.	14% ("ex-care" group) 20% (controls)
Personal and social functioning as adults.	Agency records. Interviews with 106 subjects living in Washington state.	41%

STUDY	TYPE OF STUDY	CHARACTERISTICS OF SAMPLE
Barth, R. (1990). On their own: The experiences of youth after foster care. *Child and Adolescent Social Work, 7,* 419–440.	Retrospective, no comparison group	N = 55 Ages: 17–26 Selection criteria: Youths who had left foster care in the San Francisco Bay area and Sacramento more than one year but less than 10 years prior to the study and who were at least 16 years old when emancipated. All had been on their own for at least one year.
Cook, R., Fleishman, E., & Grimes, V. (1991). *A national evaluation of Title IV-E foster care independent living programs for youth: Phase 2, Final Report Volume 1.* Rockville, MD: Westat, Inc.	Retrospective, no comparison group, some normative data provided	N = 810 Ages: 18–23 Selection criteria: Multistage, stratified design with probability sampling; youths 16 and older who were discharged 1/87 to 7/88; median time in care = 2.5 years.
Cook, S. K. (1992). Long term consequences of foster care for adult well-being. (Ph.D. dissertation), University of Nebraska, Lincoln.	Retrospective comparison of survey respondents with and without foster care history	N = 107 Ages: 19 or older Average age (foster care) = 37 years. Average time in placement = 7 years. Selection criteria: Based on the 1988 National Survey of Families and Households; national multi-stage area probability sample of 13,017 U.S. non-institutionalized adults.

Note: All Ns are final sample sizes, after attrition had taken place.

OUTCOMES STUDIED

DATA COLLECTION

Employment, contact with foster parents and biological relatives, education, life skills, health, substance use, criminal activity, housing, income.	Interviews, typically in the youths' homes (24% by phone), lasting one to three hours.	25%
Able to maintain a job at least one year; high school graduate; health care; not a cost to community; avoided young parenthood; social support; life satisfaction; overall "success."	Interviews: conducted between 11/90 to 3/91.	51%
Life happiness, depression, self-esteem, marital happiness, paternal relationship, maternal relationship, and social isolation.	Main 1988 National Survey of Families and Households survey (face-to-face interview lasting 1 hour 40 minutes on average) and self-administered supplemental survey.	Unknown for foster care subjects; overall rate of 32%

Appendix B

Studies of Outcomes of Out-of-Home Care (Summary)

McCord, McCord, and Thurber 1960

The Cambridge-Somerville (Massachusetts) Youth Study was undertaken to investigate the effectiveness of a delinquency-prevention project. It included extensive observations of the behavior, child-rearing practices, and attitudes of the families of 255 relatively lower-class, urban boys during their childhoods. Initial data collection took place between 1937 and 1945, when the youths were 9 to 17 years old.

The prospective study reported by these authors was a follow-up of the earlier project. McCord, McCord, and Thurber attempted to evaluate the long-term effectiveness of foster home placement in preventing socially deviant behavior.

During the original initiative, 24 boys were removed from their homes at the instigation of the Cambridge-Somerville staff. They all were placed in out-of-home care in their early adolescent years as a "last resort" when other social service interventions failed to stop their unacceptable behavior.

Extensive information was available about the biological families of 19 of these boys, and they became the subjects of this study. Of the other five boys, three had lived in foster homes during most of the Youth Study, and two had lived with stepmothers prior to their foster home placements; these five were excluded because of the lack of information regarding their biological families.

From the remaining sample of 236 boys in the original study, 19 were selected as a comparison group. Their early environments were similar to the "natural families" of the boys who later were placed in out-of-home care. The two groups were matched on the following factors: whether the biological father was in the home, deviance or nondeviance of the mother and father, emotional attitudes of the mother and father toward the boy, and the mother's and the father's disciplinary techniques.

In 1956 and 1957, when the subjects were in their early thirties, the authors conducted an inquiry into the degree of adult deviance among the subjects and the controls. *Deviance* included (a) criminal behavior that resulted in a conviction for assault, larceny, sexual crimes, or public drunkenness; (b) alcoholism, as determined by two or more arrests—but not convictions—for public drunkenness, commitment to a mental hospital with a diagnosis of alcoholism, membership in Alcoholics Anonymous, or seeking help from a private agency for treatment of alcoholism; and (c) psychosis, defined as the commitment to a state mental hospital with a diagnosis of schizophrenia, paranoia, or manic-depressive tendencies. Data were collected from the records of courts, mental hospitals, and social service agencies.

Specific information was not provided in this article regarding age of the subjects at placement or at follow-up, types of abuse or neglect experienced by the subjects, length of time in care, disposition from care, or special needs or disabilities.

Maas 1963

Maas retrospectively studied 20 young adults who, as preschool children in London during World War II, were placed for their safety by their parents in British wartime residential nurseries. The purpose of the investigation was to determine whether the subjects suffered "irreversible psychosocial damage" as a result of separation from their families.

All of the subjects had been in residential care for at least one year and all came from intact families without evidence of gross pathology. They had been placed in one of three wartime residential nurseries. Nursery N, located near London, had a low staff-child ratio (five to one) and encouraged the expression of the children's feelings. Nursery E, located in Wales, enrolled about 20 children with two staff members and focused on firm discipline. Nursery S, the largest nursery, took in about 47 children who had been in day nursery school together in London while their mothers worked. These 47 children and four staff members, trained teachers, moved together to a residential setting, where the emphasis was on "faith in God, King, and denial, rather inspirational and repressive and quite possessive" (p. 61). Because of the need to locate another subject who had been placed in care in infancy, one person from a fourth nursery (O) was also included in the study.

Subjects included seven young adults who had been in Nursery N, seven who had been in Nursery E, five from Nursery S, and one from Nursery O. There were 12 males and eight females. They were 19 to 26 years old at the time of the study in 1960-61; one-half were 21 years old or younger. Five of the subjects had been separated from their parents in the first year of life (Ones); five, at about 2 to 2 1/2 years of age (Twos); five, at 3 to 3 1/2 years (Threes); and five, at four to five years (Four-Pluses). Their ages at placement ranged from two to 61 months, and they were selected so that there was at least one subject from each age grouping in each nursery.

The subjects had been residents of the nurseries for a range of 12 to 50 months; the mean time spent in care was just over three years. The younger the child was at placement, the longer the stay tended to be. All of the children returned to their families while they were growing up, but two of the Ones and one of the Four-Pluses spent four or more years in a boarding school, training school, or institution for deprived children after their wartime placements. One other Four-Plus, before returning home, finished the war years in other nonrelative placements. The remaining 16 subjects grew up with their families without interruption after their wartime nursery school stays.

No control group was utilized, and Maas explains the rationale for this. First, he suggested that matched subjects would have been children who remained in London and experienced air raids; this experience would have made them very different from the nursery attenders. Second, parents who sent their children away may have been different from other parents with regard to their feelings about parental roles; matching for this characteristic would have required locating parents who had wanted to send their children away but could not for some reason, and there was no reasonable way to find such Londoners.

The subjects were interviewed, and 14 of them were observed in interactions with various family members. Interviews centered on their living arrangements throughout their lives, employment, leisure-time interests, education, and family life. They also were given the TAT (Thematic Apperception Test); five males and five females also completed the California Psychological Inventory, but Maas did not report their scores.

In addition, parents of 18 of the subjects were interviewed; they were asked about the circumstances surrounding their children's leaving and homecoming and about their current adjustment. Records of collateral agencies—children's departments, medical facilities, etc.—were consulted; data from these sources basically confirmed the reports of the subjects. Based upon the material collected from all of the sources, ratings for each subject were assigned for the following areas: feeling life, inner controls, relationships with others, performance of key social roles, and intellectual functioning.

Meier 1965

Meier studied 66 former foster children who had grown up in Minnesota. The respondents were 28 to 32 years old at the time of the study, had experienced five years or more of family foster care in their childhood, had not been returned to their own families while children, and were discharged from guardianship between July 1, 1948, and December 31, 1949. All of the eligible males ($N = 34$) and a random sample of 48 of the eligible 64 females were included in the study sample; two of the 82 people had died, five were not located, and nine refused to participate.

Over half of the subjects had left home before the age of five. They had been in care for an average of 11 years and 10 months, and the average age at discharge was 18 years, one month. Complete information was collected from one African American and 65 Caucasian.

Data were collected from interviews with 61 subjects and questionnaires from five more. In addition, a limited amount of information was collected via phone calls or letters from subjects who had refused to participate in the full study. The subjects' social effectiveness and sense of well-being were assessed and related to particular factors in family foster care (e.g., age at placement and number of placements). Effectiveness and well-being were measured using variables pertaining to family life, living arrangements, economic and employment history, and community involvement.

Allerhand, Weber, and Haug 1966

A group of 50 boys who had been clients of Bellefaire, a residential treatment facility for emotionally disturbed children in Cleveland, Ohio, were located one to two years after discharge and agreed to participate in this study. The authors were interested in measuring their post-discharge adaptation and relating it to a variety of placement and care variables.

The potential subjects were all boys who had been in care at Bellefaire at least six months and had been discharged between January 1958 and June 1961; two of the 52 youths who met the criteria refused to participate. The mean age of the subjects at entry into care was just under 13 years (range of 5 years, 11 months to 16 years, 6 months), and the average length of stay was 3.5 years (range of six months to 6.5 years).

Assessments of the subjects, using scales developed for the study, were made three months after admission, 15 months after admission, at discharge, and one to two years after discharge. Six major kinds of data were collected: "hard" or factual information, adaptability levels, casework variables, situational variables at follow-up, staff evaluations of the child's problems and progress while in care, and the child's actual behavior.

Data were collected from agency records and interviews with the subjects, their parents or parent substitutes, and their therapists if they were still in treatment.

Ferguson 1966

This Scottish study sought to discover how a series of young people who had been in care in the Children's Department in Glasgow had fared after they left school and then left care at 18. Included in the investigation were foster youths who reached the age of 18 between 1961 and 1963. They lived in a variety of types of placements: 16% with relatives or already-functioning guardians, 13% in residential homes, 56% with foster families following brief stays in residential facilities, 12% directly with foster families, 2% in "Training Hostels," and one in "lodgings."

Of the 205 potential subjects (110 males and 95 females) who were approached, 203 agreed to participate. Twenty-six percent of the potential subjects entered care as infants, 39% between one and four years of age, 22% between five and nine, 12% between 10 and 14, and 2% at age 15. The sources of data were agency file information, school teachers' reports, and interviews with the subjects every six months for two years after discharge.

Outcomes measured included scholastic achievement, health and recreation, criminal behavior, employment, family life, and migration to other communities. Two comparisons were made, first with a 1947 study of 1,349 Glasgow males who left school at age 14, and then with a study of 400 Glasgow females who left school at 15 in 1961.

Heston, Denney, and Pauly 1966

This retrospective study compares 47 adults who had been placed in foundling homes in Oregon with 50 adults who either were never in child care institutions or had experienced less than three months of such care. The subjects were selected from the records of a previous study designed to test the genetic contribution to schizophrenia by comparing children born to schizophrenic mothers with control children, where both groups had been reared apart from their biological mothers.

The subjects were divided into four groups: (A) 25 subjects born to schizophrenic mothers in Oregon state psychiatric hospitals and cared for in foundling homes pending adoption or other out-of-home placement; (B) 22 subjects born to parents with no known history of psychiatric disorder who were cared for in the same foundling homes; they were matched with subjects from group A for gender, type of disposition (adoption or foster home), and length of stay in the foundling home; (C) 22 subjects born to schizophrenic mothers in Oregon state psychiatric hospitals but not placed in foundling homes; most were reared in the homes of paternal relatives; (D) 28 subjects born to parents with no known psychiatric history and chosen to match group C; they had spent less than three months in foundling homes and most were reared by relatives. Participants in group A and B were known as the institutional group, while those in C and D were named the "family group."

The subjects, all Caucasian, had been born between 1915 and 1945, and all apparently had been normal at birth. They had been separated permanently from their biological mothers after the first few postpartum days and eventually had been placed in homes where both parental figures were represented (except for a few who stayed in foundling homes for more than five years). The subjects were between ages of 21 and 50 years old when they were studied in 1964 and 1965. The average age of the institutional group was 34 years, and that of the Family group was 38 years. Thirty-five percent of the subjects were female and 65% male; the proportion was about the same in both groups.

The original sample of schizophrenic-mother subjects numbered 74; 16 of them were dropped from the study because of death, contact with their biological mother or her relatives, severe physical problems, or a lack of an appropriate control subject. Fifty-eight subjects not born to schizophrenic mothers were chosen to match those remaining from the original group; they were matched on the basis of gender, type of eventual placement (adoption, family foster home, institution), and length of time in child care institutions. Of the 116 people in the two groups, 14 had died in infancy or childhood and 5 could not be found. Attrition was not significantly different for the Institutional and Family groups.

All those in the institutional group had been admitted to foundling homes within the first few days of life. Fourteen subjects spent 3 to 12 months in the homes, 13 stayed for 12 to 24 months, eight for 24 to 36 months, four for 36 to 48 months, one for 48 to 60 months, and seven more than 60 months. The average stay was 25 months. The authors state the these figures underestimate the time spent in care, for 10 people were known to have been readmitted to the same or other foundling homes, and several had lived in more than one family foster home. In contrast, subjects in the family group changed homes infrequently.

Follow-up data were collected through interviews with 72 subjects (33 "institutionals" and 39 "families") and, for all participants, from records of hospitals, schools, police, the Veterans' Administration, and the armed forces. MMPI scores for 78 subjects were derived from testing completed during interviews or from their records. Socioeconomic status was estimated at two points in time: the status of the first home in which the child was placed and the status at the time of follow-up. Each subject was also assigned a numerical score (range of 0 to 100) for the level of psychosocial disability; the scoring was based upon the Menninger Mental Health Sickness Rating Scale (MHSRS). A psychiatric diagnosis was made if indicated; the diagnoses used were schizophrenia, sociopathy, mental deficiency, or "neurotic personality disorder" (corresponding to a score on the MHSRS of less than 75 and a diagnosis other than the first three categories).

A companion study by Heston [1966] utilized the same data to differentiate outcomes for subjects born of schizophrenic mothers from those of subjects born to women without that diagnosis. This analysis found significantly more indications of psychosocial disability among the former group.

Robins 1966

Robins compared the adult status of 524 former child guidance clinic patients with that of 100 nonpatient subjects. The purpose of this longitudinal investigation was to describe the "natural history" of the sociopathic personality.

The experimental group was chosen from among patients seen at the St. Louis Municipal Psychiatric Clinic between January 1, 1924, and December 30, 1929. All had been under 18 years of age at referral, had IQs of at least 80, and had histories of emotional or behavioral problems; omitted were patients with no social histories in their files and African Americans (owing to their small number).

This selection process yielded a group of 524 former patients, about 20% of all of the cases seen at the clinic during that time. Sixteen percent had lived in family foster homes and 16% in orphanages for six months or more before their referral to the clinic; 9% had been placed in public correctional or private semi-correctional institutions, and 1% each had been placed in hospitals and mental hospitals. Twenty-eight percent of the males and 47% of the females had lived in an institution or family foster home by the time they were referred. Their median age at the time of referral was 13 years, with a range of 18 months to 17 years. At the time of referral, 51% were at least one year behind in school performance.

The 100 control subjects were selected from public elementary school records and were matched with the experimental group for race, gender, age, and neighborhood in which they lived during the 1920s. They were Caucasian, had IQs of at least 80, had attended St. Louis elementary schools for at least two years, had no record of expulsion from school or transfer to correctional institutions, and had not repeated as much as a full year of elementary school. Former students meeting these criteria were chosen randomly from microfilm reels of school records until the selection quotas were filled.

The experimental group was 27% female, compared with 30% of the control group. The article did not provide information regarding the ages of the subjects at the time of the study. However, calculations using the ages at referral and the number of years between referral and follow-up suggest that the potential age range was 27 to 53 years with a mean of about 44 years. The controls had grown up in families with higher financial status than the others; their IQs appeared to be higher, but this may be a result of the use of different tests for the two groups. Two percent of the controls and 50% of the patients had appeared in juvenile court; an additional 10%

of the former and 15% of the latter had police records as children.

An attempt was made to interview every surviving subject and at least one close relative of any subject who had died at the age of 25 or later. Four percent of the patients and 1% of the controls had died before 25; these 23 subjects were eliminated from the study, leaving a total target group of 601. Nine percent of the patients and 8% of the controls were known to have died after 25. Ninety percent of the total subjects—88% of the patients and 98% of the controls—were either located or else known to have died. Interviews were completed between 1955 and 1960 for 491 participants: 80% of the former patients and 90% of the controls. Four hundred sixteen (85%) of the interviews were with subjects themselves, and 75 were with relatives; 49 of the latter were with relatives of deceased subjects; the rest were with relatives of living subjects.

Target subjects interviewed totaled 110: six were in mental hospitals and considered uninterviewable; 52 were not located; four were dead and no relative was available for the interview; five were located but not approached because they lived far away or were found too late for inclusion; and 43 refused to participate. Initially, even more subjects had refused to be interviewed; 27% of these later agreed to be studied. Those subjects who initially had refused to participate differed from those who cooperated in several ways: they had completed fewer years of schooling, were less often engaged in professional occupations, were less likely to have American-born parents, and were more often St. Louis residents.

The interviews were based upon a structured set of questions. Areas covered included an evaluation of the childhood home, school problems and achievement, marital history, adult relationships with family members, other social relationships, military service, job history, history of arrests and incarcerations, financial dependency, geographic moves, history of deviant behavior, physical and psychiatric diseases, and alcohol and drug use. Interviewers evaluated the subjects on their intellectual level, cooperativeness, willingness to talk, frankness, and mood.

In addition to the interviews, information was collected from other sources. The records of a variety of organizations were reviewed: schools, courts and law enforcement agencies, probation and parole offices, reformatories and penitentiaries, the Social Service Exchange, credit rating bureaus, medical and psychiatric hospitals, the Armed Forces Record Center, the Social Security Administration, local welfare agencies, and coroners' offices.

Maas 1969

"Children in Long Term Foster Care" reports the results of a follow-up of Maas and Engler's 1959 study *Children in Need of Parents*. The original 551 respondents were a random sample of children in out-of-home care in nine counties around the United States. They had been placed in either family foster care or institutions as of April 1, 1957, and had been in care for at least three months. The authors predicted that over half of the children would remain in care "for ten or so years," based upon the frequency of parental visits and the parents' plans regarding their children.

The 1969 article describes the findings of a follow-up investigation conducted in 1967, which tested the accuracy of the prediction of the original study 10 years later. Agencies in eight of the nine initial counties agreed to participate in the follow-up by completing questionnaires pertaining to the dispositions of those formerly in care as children. These agencies had cared for 480 of the original sample, and usable returns were received for 422 of them. Of these, 35 were still in care in 1967, and the disposition of six others was not known.

An additional investigation of 25 of "the most extreme cases of long-term care" was conducted; these subjects had been placed in care within the first two years of life and had remained in care until late adolescence.

Data were collected regarding: (1) a variety of placement variables, such as length of time in care and parental visits and plans; (2) certain child and family variables, such as the nature of the family relationships and the child's physical and intellectual development; (3) agency factors, such as the level of treatment received and workers' relationships with family members; and (4) the nature of the disposition of the case. The information was used to determine whether specific factors might predict length of time in care.

Frommer and O'Shea 1973a, 1973b

These authors participated in a project that attempted to identify at antenatal clinics in London mothers who might be vulnerable for having problems with their children in the future. One variable which they studied was whether or not the mother had been separated from her own parent(s) when she was a child. The study included both retrospective and prospective methodologies.

All subjects were married, British-born, primigravidae women who were attending any one of three antenatal clinics of St. Thomas' Hospital's Department of Obstetrics during April to June 1969. Their expected delivery dates were between May and December of that year. The women were divided into two groups based upon whether they reported on an initial questionnaire that they had been separated from one or both parents before the age of 11. *Separation* was operationalized as having had at least one parent die or having experienced an event which necessitated that the child or one or both of her parents sleep away from home. The data analysis did not separate out those women who had been "in care."

All separated subjects who agreed to participate were accepted into the study. Controls were chosen from those reporting no separations and were matched with the separated subjects by age, social class, and expected date of delivery. For the inquiry reported in the 1973b article, the women were further subdivided into those who had had more than one minor management problem with the infant during the first year of the child's life or had had marital problems, or both, and those with no marital problems and at worst one minor infant-management problem.

A questionnaire that sought agreement to participate and identification of those women who had experienced separation from their parents was presented to all women who met the criteria ($N = 220$). Nineteen women (9%) refused to participate in the project. Of the remaining 201 potential subjects, 59 had been separated and 142 had not. Initially, 58 pairs of women were matched; 10 controls either moved or miscarried soon after matching, and most were replaced. Before the part of the study reported in the 1973a article was completed, 13 separated subjects and 14 additional controls dropped out, leaving 45 separated women and 44 non-separated women in the project. Between the initial matching and the completion of the first phase of the study, a total of 20 controls and 13 separated women left the project; 15 of the former and seven of the latter were considered refusers, leaving an overall refusal rate of 19%. (The presentation in the report of the numbers of subjects at various stages of the process was somewhat confusing; the information above is as accurate as is possible under the circumstances.)

The 1973b article presented a further follow-up of the 89 participants described above. Only 79 of these women, however, could be visited at that time: 40 of the original separated group and 39 of the controls. By this time, it had been discovered that 23 of the control subjects actually had experienced a childhood separation and that the separations of two of the separated women had occurred after age 11. Eight subgroups resulted from the divisions of the subjects in this second analysis. Among the 40 women originally in the separated group, there were separated women with problems (number not reported), separated women without problems (number not reported), nonseparated women with problems ($n = 0$), and nonseparated women (i.e., separated after age 11) without problems ($n = 2$). Among the 39 women in the control group, there were nonseparated women with problems ($n = 5$), nonseparated women without problems ($n = 11$), separated women who originally had denied a separation experience with problems ($n = 18$), and separated women who originally had denied a separation experience without problems ($n = 5$).

The first article presents the findings generated from a one-year (post-birth) follow-up. The women were interviewed antenatally when possible, and then when the infant was two to three months old, six to seven months old, 9 to 10 months old, and 12 to 13 months old. The final analysis of the data included only those subjects seen for three or more postnatal interviews.

Women who were interviewed before their child's birth completed a questionnaire pertaining to their attitudes toward pregnancy, plans for the baby, their own health, and the expected financial impact of having a baby. The postnatal interviews included questions about the woman's feelings toward her child and husband, her state of subjective physical and mental health, housing, and behavior of the infant (sleeping, crying, feeding, temperament, and achievement of developmental milestones). In addition, the interviewer observed the mother's manner of coping with her baby.

The follow-up reported in the second article [1973b] involved an additional interview with 79 subjects; the postnatal timing of this phase of the project was not reported. The participants were asked about problems they had had with their marriages or with their babies, the atmosphere in which they grew up, how their parents related to each other and to them, and the nature of their relationships with their fathers or father-substitutes.

Palmer 1976

Palmer examined the progress of children in long-term care, looking for associations between the progress they made and their experiences before and during care. The subjects (N = 200) had been recipients of long-term care in one of three Children's Aid Society agencies abroad, two in Toronto, and one in London. The criteria for acceptance into the study were that the subject was age three or older at the time of placement; spent a minimum of five years (not necessarily continuously) in care, ending when the child reached majority; did not have physical or mental conditions so extreme as to prevent leading a normal life; and was not from a distinct minority.

All of those who met the criteria in London were included as subjects (n = 70), as were 130 of the possible 300 Toronto children whose case files were not out of their offices being microfilmed. The author states that about 10% of London and 5% of Toronto cases lacked enough information regarding the biological family to be accepted, but it is not clear whether these cases are part of the group of 200 subjects or of the original 370 cases.

The children's case files were examined to retrieve data regarding progress while in care, with "progress" being divided into two categories: behavioral, emotional, or task performance problems; and academic progress. Associations were sought between these areas and placement and background variables, such as age at separation from parents, intelligence, gender, number of placements, experiences with the biological family, preparation for placement, parental contacts, placement with siblings, identification with biological or foster families, training of the worker, and socioeconomic level of the foster parents.

Wolkind 1977a; 1977b

Wolkind selected and studied a group of women whose background and social circumstances might predict "an increased risk of difficulties arising in their future maternal role" [1977b: 179]. One background factor that he identified was the experience of having been in care as a child. The sample included all women with the following characteristics: over the age of 16, born in Britain, possessing a permanent address in an inner-London borough, expecting their first baby, and attending the obstetric clinic of a hospital in the borough during a one-year period.

Interviews were completed with 534 women; four other women refused to participate, and the author estimated that about 20 pregnant women in the borough were missed because they received prenatal care elsewhere. About 95% of the women who met the selection criteria were interviewed.

The interviews included questions regarding the women's childhood experiences, history of housing or social problems, their and their husbands' psychiatric and chronic physical disorders, their attitudes toward their health in pregnancy, and the circumstances surrounding any admissions to local-authority care that occurred before the age of 16 and that lasted one month or more. Psychiatric disorders were identified based upon evidence of treatment from general practitioners or psychiatrists for any form of psychiatric disturbance in the two years before the interview. The women also completed the "Malaise Inventory," a brief self-rating questionnaire from the Cornell Medical Index, in which they described their usual state of health prior to their pregnancies.

Thirty-six of the subjects (7%) described at least one episode of having been in the care of the local authority for at least one month. Thirteen of these had entered care before the age of five years; 23 had been in care for at least one year. The reasons reported for admission into care were family breakup, 33%; parental illness, 17%; "child" factors, 14%;

parental death, 11%; homelessness, 3%; and unknown, 22%. The dispositions of placements were not described.

Fanshel and Shinn 1978

Children in Foster Care: A Longitudinal Investigation was a ground-breaking study of 624 children who entered New York City's out-of-home care system in 1966 and remained in care at least 90 days. The full-time substitute living arrangements used by the subjects included family foster homes, institutions for dependent or neglected children, group homes, and residential treatment centers for emotionally disturbed children. The subjects had never been in placement before, nor had they had a sibling in placement; they were no more than 12 years old at the time of admission into care. In the study, 467 family groups were represented; 157 families had two children represented.

Quotas for age and gender were established, and subjects who met the criteria were accepted in order of appearance until the quotas were filled. The study included 75 infants (birth to six months), 100 toddlers (six months to two years), 175 preschoolers (two to six years), and 250 subjects in mid-childhood (6 to 12 years). The percentage who were male was 50.6. Twenty-one percent were Caucasian Catholics or Protestants, 5% were Jewish, 31% were African American Protestants, 11% were African American Catholics, and 32% were Puerto Ricans or other Latinos. The subjects represented about one-fourth of the children admitted into care from January through August 1966.

The personal and social adjustment of the subjects, as well as the status changes they experienced, were studied over a five-year period, utilizing several forms of data collection: intelligence and projective testing, behavioral ratings and developmental profiles, teachers' assessments, parental reports, and the self-report of older children. Measurements were made at three points in time: within 90 days of entry, 2.5 years after entry, and 5 years after entry.

Fox and Arcuri 1980

In 1978, the Children's Aid Society of Pennsylvania (CAS) surveyed the school-aged foster children in its care with specific attention to their level of cognitive and academic skills. The authors hypothesized that, due to the past experiences of the foster children, their functional levels would be below those of poverty-level children living with their own families. If this were not found to be the case, it might be evidence that "ameliorative influences" were operating in out-of-home care settings.

Children under the care of CAS completed psychological testing at intake and at various intervals during their placement. The sample for this study consisted of all children seen for testing in 1978, a total of 163 children aged 4 years, 11 months to 18 years, 1 month (mean of 9.6 years). There were 93 males and 70 females; 136 were African American and 27 were Caucasian.

The children's placement ages ranged from newborn to 14.9 years, the average age at placement was 4.3 years. On average, the participants had been in the care of CAS for 5.2 years; the time in care ranged from a few days to almost 16 years. Each subject had experienced between one and six placements, with the "usual history" involving two placements, one on an emergency basis and one long-term. Reasons for placement of the children included parental incompetence or unavailability, 69%; abuse or gross neglect, 27%; and the child's own behavior or medical problems, 6%. These percentages total 102; the source of the error is not known.

Wechsler Intelligence Tests were given to all subjects; the authors acknowledged that these tests were biased in favor of Caucasian, middle-class children. The Preschool and Primary

Scale was administered to 27; 133 took the Children-Revised version; and three were given the Adult Scale. School achievement scores were obtained from the WRAT (Wide Range Achievement Test); 140 participants took the WRAT-Reading test (the skills of 23 were at the preprimary level), which measures word recognition, and 57 took the WRAT-Arithmetic test. Grade placement data were also collected.

Harari 1980

Harari conducted a study of former foster children in California who had not returned to their parents upon exiting from care, usually at the age of 18 or upon becoming emancipated minors. The objectives of the project were to determine the perceptions of placement workers and teenagers/young adults of the importance of various offered, used, and needed out-of-home care services; to conduct an assessment of the subjects' interpersonal affect and self-esteem; and to explore the extent to which the perceptions of out-of-home care service providers can serve as predictors for post-out-of-home care adjustment. There were three hypotheses: (1) that placement workers and teenagers/young adults will have different perceptions of services offered, used, and needed; (2) that these two groups will differ in their perception of the importance of various services; and (3) that certain perceptions may serve as significant predictors for post-out-of-home care adjustment.

The subjects were 34 young people who had left family foster care in a county in northern California as adolescents and did not return to their parents at that time. The initial sample included teenagers who had left family foster care, where they were under the auspices of the welfare department, between 1974 and 1978; they had been in care for a minimum of 1.5 years and had never been diagnosed as mentally retarded. No control group of adolescents never having been in out-of-home care was used.

About 259 adolescents who were 18 by February 1978

had left family foster care between January 1974 and June 1978; 85 fit the criteria described and still lived in northern California. These 85 potential subjects were sent letters requesting their participation; they were offered $7.00 for an interview. Twenty-one letters were returned because the subjects had moved; 22 of the young people did not respond to the letter; four refused to participate; and 38 agreed to participate. Of these 38, interviews were conducted with 34 subjects between July and November 1978; two potential subjects were found to be living in group care, one responded too late to be included, and one never confirmed an appointment time.

Of the respondents, 77% were women; 74 were Caucasian, 9% were African American, 8.8% had Spanish surnames, 6% were Eurasian, and 3% were Asian. Their average age was 19.8 years, with a range of 17 to 23 years at the time of the interviews.

The participants had experienced an average of three placements each, the average for all California children in out-of-home care. There was a range of 1 to 11 different foster placements. The average age of the children at entry into care was 10.3 years; 6% entered during the first year of life, 15% between the ages of 1 and 5, 18% between the ages of 5 and 10, 29% between 10 and 13, and 32% between 13 and 16.

The young people had been in care an average of 7.3 years; 9% were in care for 1 to 2 years; 27% for 2 to 4 years; 29% for 4 to 7 years; 15% for 7 to 11 years; 6% for 11 to 15 years; and 15% for 15 to 19 years. The reasons for leaving care were varied: 53% because they reached the age of 18 or became emancipated minors, 18% because they married, 6% because they were placed with relatives, 3% because they quit school or vocational training, and 21% for other reasons (problems with foster parents, medical problems, assignment of a guardian, problems with a social worker, and joining the army).

The workers who were invited to participate in the study included all placement workers and their supervisors from the county being studied and workers who had moved to other positions or departments but had been placement workers between 1974 and 1978. A total of 47 placement workers and supervisors participated.

The interview schedule for subjects included both open and closed questions regarding perceptions of the out-of-home care experience and current life circumstances. In addition, they completed three service list forms and two scales from the Jackson Personality Inventory (JPI). The service list asked how often each of 10 out-of-home care services was offered, used, or needed. The two JPI scales were Interpersonal Affect—the ability to be intimate and to show concern for others—and Self-Esteem—self-confidence in interpersonal situations. Each scale had 20 true-false questions.

Workers also completed three service list forms. They were asked how often the "typical child in foster family care" was offered, made use of, and needed each of 10 out-of-home care services.

Triseliotis 1980

The aim of "Growing Up in Foster Care and After" was to learn about the long-term out-of-home care experience in Scotland as seen through the eyes of foster parents and children formerly in care. The current social and personal circumstances of those formerly in care as children were examined and related back to certain of their background characteristics and experiences. Outcomes that were studied included the nature of foster child-foster parent relationships, satisfaction with the out-of-home care experience, educational achievement, employment history, family life, contact with the former foster family, living arrangements, coping ability, sense of well-being, criminal behavior, and perceptions of social workers.

Out of a potential sample of 59, 40 subjects participated in this project; all had been born in 1956 or 1957 and had spent 7 to 15 years each in a single family foster home before the age of 16. The subjects and their former foster parents were interviewed during 1976 and 1977. They were 20 to 21 years at the time of the interviews and had spent an average of 12 years in a single family foster home; many also had had other shorter placements.

Kraus 1981

Kraus's work is part of a broad ongoing investigation into the long-term effects of out-of-home care in Australia. Long-term effects were defined as "those effects of fostering that manifest themselves in the personal and social functioning of former foster children as adults" (p. 100). This particular inquiry explored the relationship between adult criminal activity and two placement variables: length of time in care and number of different out-of-home placements.

The sample consisted of all former wards of the state in New South Wales who were born in 1951 or 1952 and discharged from supervision upon reaching their 18th birthday into situations other than the care of their family or relatives. Because of the selection criteria, the author considered the sample to present a "higher social risk" than the population of former wards generally. Kraus deliberately "maximized the functional significance of foster care, because in this sample such care was not a transient episode but a transitional phase from dependence on natural family to social independence" (p. 101).

There were 246 males and 245 females in the sample; this group constituted 50% of all state wards whose supervision was terminated during 1969 or 1970. They were 27 to 28 years old at the time of the study. Their time in care ranged from two months to just under 18 years; the mean was 9.3 years. For purposes of analysis, time in care was dichotomized between those who spent up to 8 years, 11 months in placement, and those placed for 9 years or more.

The subjects had between one and nine different placements each. Of those who had been in family foster homes, 56% of the males and 54% of the females had been in one or two different homes; 33% of the males and 36% of the females had been in three to five homes; and 11% of the males and 10% of the females had six to nine placements. Seventeen of the wards had never been placed in a family foster home, and seven had an unknown history of placements.

Records of the former Child Welfare Department of New South Wales were used to obtain the birth cohort and relevant information regarding the length of state wardship under a "care and protection court order" and the number of foster placements during that period. "Foster placement" was defined as family foster care only, excluding group homes. Criminal records of the subjects from their 18th birthday until December 15, 1979, were traced through the New South Wales Police, which had records for all of Australia and recorded all convictions except those for traffic and driving offenses.

The author noted a particular limitation of the analysis. There is a strong correlation between the variables of the reason for commitment into care, length of time in care, and age at entering care. This confounding of preexisting conditions and the care experiences limits the interpretation of the study's findings. Another limitation is imposed by the dichotomizing of data, which results in the loss of some data.

Zimmerman 1982

The purpose of *Foster Care in Retrospect* was to determine the current circumstances of young adults who had lived in foster homes in New Orleans under the auspices of the Orleans Parish Department of Public Welfare for all or part of their childhood. In addition, this descriptive, exploratory study sought feedback regarding the nature and quality of the out-of-home care experience and the identification of factors in childhood that appeared to be related to the subjects' current functioning.

The initial sample was defined as those young adults currently 18 to 28 years old who had been in out-of-home care under the auspices of the above-named department for at least four months during their childhood; this produced a sample of 319 cases, which was reduced by choosing only one child from each family, rotating the birth order of the child chosen. Additional selection criteria were then added: the subjects had to have been in a foster home for at least one year, could not have been placed for adoption, and could not have been placed in a distant state that made the young person difficult to locate. This further reduced the potential sample to 170 subjects, 65% of whom ($N = 109$) were located. Forty-eight of these did not participate in the research: 20 refused; seven were institutionalized or handicapped in some way; eight were living out of state on their own; two had died; and 11 did not participate for other reasons.

Of the final sample of 61 subjects who were interviewed, 53% were male and 47% were female; 51% were ages 24 to 29 when interviewed, and 49% were 19 to 23; 66% were black and 34% were Caucasian. The average age at their first out-of-home care placement was three to four years; 63% entered care under the age of six. Fifty-six percent of the subjects left care when they were 15 to 21 years old; 26% left between the ages of three and eight; and 18% left between 9 and 14.

Outcomes studied included the subjects' family life, living arrangements, educational achievement, employment and income, social supports, health, leisure time, criminal behavior, satisfaction with life, and voting behavior.

Festinger 1983

The goals of *No One Ever Asked Us* were twofold: (1) to provide a detailed picture of certain aspects of the lives of a group of young adults who had been discharged from out-of-home care upon or after reaching the age of majority, and (2) to obtain their views on the out-of-home care experience and what might be done to improve it. Potential subjects were people who had been discharged from out-of-home care in the New York City metropolitan area in 1975, who had been in care continuously for at least the preceding five years, and who were 18 to 21 years old at discharge.

Of a potential sample of over 600, 277 people participated in the study; 186 were interviewed in person, 55 were interviewed by telephone, and 36 completed questionnaires. The data were collected between May 1979 and April 1980. Forty-two percent of the respondents were female and 58% male; 52% were African American, 28% were Caucasian, 19% were Latino, and 1% were Oriental. Thirty-five percent of the subjects were Protestant, 33% were Catholic, 6% were Jewish, 10% were oriented to various other religions, and 15% claimed no religious affiliation.

A wide variety of outcomes were examined, among them the respondents' sense of well-being, contact with kin and former foster families, personal problems, social and family support systems, educational achievement, financial status, employment history, condition of health, drug and alcohol use, history of criminal behavior, use of formal help providers, and perceptions of the care experience. Where possible, comparisons were made on these outcome variables with responses from people of the same age group who participated in three general population surveys.

Frost and Jurich 1983

This unpublished retrospective study was conducted in part to investigate the functioning of past residents of The Villages in Topeka, Kansas, in order to assess the impact of the care received in these group homes and to evaluate the effectiveness of this program. The Villages provides long-term residential surrogate family care for abused and neglected children between the ages of 6 and 18.

The potential subjects all had lived in group care at The Villages for at least six months and had graduated from the program by October 1, 1982. Within a population of 176 graduates, 96 persons participated in the research: 57 males and 39 females (the potential sample included 89 males and 87 females). Three past residents had died and six refused to be interviewed; the remaining graduates had not yet been reached when the report was written.

Twenty-six percent of the sample were between the ages of 6 and 11 when they entered The Villages; 34% were 12 to 14 years old, and 40% were 15 or older. Seventeen percent had had no prior placements, 32% had had one, 36% had had two or three, and 15% had had four or more. The following lengths of stay were found: 6 to 12 months, 20%; 13 to 24 months, 25%; 25 to 36 months, 22%; and over 37 months, 33%. Over half (53%) of the subjects had left care at the age of 17 or 18; 27% were 15 to 16 years old at departure, 14% were 12 to 14 years old, and 6% were 6 to 11. The reasons for leaving The Villages were varied: 41% graduated successfully from the program, 19% returned to their own homes, 16% ran away, 15% were moved to a more structured environment, 8% entered family foster care, and 1% were adopted.

Participants completed either a personal or telephone interview or a written questionnaire in 1982 or 1983. In addition, information was collected from their files, from current and former Villages houseparents, and from the office support staff.

An interview rating scale was used to measure each subject's functioning level; the scale originally consisted of seven points (ranging from -3 to +3) but was later collapsed to create a three-point scale. The rating was based upon personal characteristics of the subjects, such as educational achievement, employment history and financial stability, relationship formation, criminal behavior, contact with welfare offices, and types of hobbies or other activities. The participants' scores on this scale were compared with certain placement variables, such as length of time in care and age at which they entered the child welfare system. The young people also were asked about their satisfaction with the care received.

This study included no control or comparison group. Tables which described the relationships between variables in terms of frequencies and percentages were included in the report, but significance levels had not been calculated; thus, the conclusions drawn were rather impressionistic. However, the report is preliminary, and further analysis of this and additional data is being conducted. This should result in a more revealing—statistically speaking—publication of findings in the near future.

Jones and Moses 1984

West Virginia's Former Foster Children explored the adjustment into the community and adult functioning of 328 persons formerly in care as children. All of these young adults had received out-of-home care in West Virginia for at least one year after October 1, 1977, and all had been discharged prior to January 1, 1984, and were at least 19 years old as of that date.

Of a total of 629 possible participants, 328 were involved in the research; 89% of these had personal interviews, 7% were interviewed by telephone, and 4% completed questionnaires. They were between the ages of 19 and 28, with a mean age of 20 years. Forty-eight percent were female and 52% male; 92% were Caucasian and 8% African American. The questions to which they responded addressed approximately the same issues as were covered in the Festinger study (see page 198).

Rest and Watson 1984

"Growing Up in Foster Care" describes a small sample of adults who grew up in long-term out-of-home care under the supervision of the Chicago Child Care Society. The Society serves an inner-city population and incorporates into its program supportive counseling services for its children in care. Potential subjects had entered the care of the Society at age six or younger, had reached adulthood within the agency's program, and were discharged between 1966 and 1981. Seventy people met these criteria, 13 of whom were nonrandomly selected to participate in the study.

The participants were 19 to 31 years of age; the median age was 25. They had been out of care for an average of five years; the range was one month to 12 years. There were nine males and four females, eight African Americans and five Caucasians. There was no control group for this sample, of which the original 70 were described by the researchers as being "small, accidental, and reflect[ing] the experience of only one agency" (p. 96).

All of the participants completed a two-to-three hour interview in 1981. Three areas were explored: their current functioning, the significance of the out-of-home care experience in childhood and its influence on their present lives, and their judgments and conclusions about their experiences. Specific outcome variables included educational and employment histories, nature of their family life, contact with kin, and self-concept.

Triseliotis and Russell 1984

The authors of *Hard to Place* initiated their research "to establish whether aspects of behavior, handicaps or difficulties are transmitted from one generation to the next in situations where children are separated from their families of origin at an early stage" (p. 15). They also were interested in more general long-term effects of discontinuities of care, early institutionalization, and placement moves on children who experienced different forms of substitute care. This study contrasted the experiences of a group of hard-to-place adoptees with a group of children placed in residential institutions.

The potential sample was drawn from past clients of social work departments and a large voluntary placement agency in Scotland. Selection criteria included having highly disadvantaged backgrounds; if an adoptee, having been placed in the adoption home between the ages of 2 and 10; if formerly in a residential institution, having been placed in one or more residential establishments when less than 10 years old and staying there at least until the age of 16; and if possible, being in one's twenties at the time of the interview. Ninety-one adoptees were in the original sample, of which 44 were interviewed; they had spent an average of 11 years and 8 months with their adoptive families before the age of 17. Forty out of the original 68 potential subjects in institutional care were interviewed; they had lived for an average of 11 years in one or more institutions. Sixty-four percent of the adoptees and 38% of those who had been in institutions were male. The mean ages at the time of the interviews were 24 years for adoptees and 22.8 years for those who had lived in institutions.

Aside from interviews, most of which were conducted from 1978 to 1980, data were collected from agency records; this was especially helpful for comparing the subjects' circumstances with those of their biological families. The authors compared their findings whenever possible with data regarding former foster children in Scotland that were collected in 1979 to 1980 by one of the authors (Triseliotis [1980]; see page 194). Outcome variables were similar to those of other studies: employment, living arrangements, mental health problems, education, financial status, health status, quality of relationships, family life, housing, criminal behavior, alcohol abuse, coping abilities, and satisfaction with life.

Dumaret 1985

The subjects of this study were children abandoned with "a view to adoption" by 28 French mothers from a disadvantaged social background. This investigation analyzed the influence of different familial and social environments on IQ, school performance, and deviant behavior in school.

The major question of the study was "What are the medium- and long-term effects of the type of placement on the siblings or half-siblings adopted or remaining in their lower-class families or raised in institutions or foster families?" (p. 554). The major hypotheses were: (1) early placement in adoptive families exerts positive effects on cognitive and social development and on school achievement—children who experience markedly different environments will have different IQs, school success, and behavior; and (2) children who live in stable families perform better than those in unstable families, even in a disadvantaged social background.

The participants included all of the offspring of 28 mothers. At least one child per mother was in both of the following groups: (1) abandoned at birth and adopted into environments of high socio-professional status, i.e., managerial and professional classes ("A" subjects described below); and (2) raised in their biological families of low socio-professional status, i.e., skilled workers, or semiskilled workers ("B" subjects below) or placed in foster families or reared in institutions ("C" subjects below).

The selection criteria resulted in three groups of subjects: A: children who were adopted and raised in a privileged social environment; B: children who remained with their biological families in a disadvantaged social environment; and C: those who were removed from their original environment after a family breakup and raised under the care of the child welfare authorities.

The children in group A ($N = 35$) had been born between 1962 and 1969; they had been abandoned before the age of one month (average age of eight days) and placed for adoption before the age of seven months (average of 4.4 months) with parents of high socio-professional status. They were selected from lists of children registered for adoption by state social welfare agencies. Twenty-two were female and 13 were male; six had North African fathers. Three sets of twins and 30 adoptive families are represented in this group.

The 48 children in group B were born between 1949 and

1970; 28 were females. Nineteen were illegitimate at birth. The 21 children in group C consisted of 7 females and 14 males. They had been born between 1953 and 1968.

All of the descendents of the 28 women were found. Data were collected pertaining to each of these children between approximately 1975 and 1980 (the exact dates were not reported); neither the subjects nor their mothers knew that they were being studied. The types of data included the Collective Scale of Intellectual Level (ECNI)—Verbal, Performance, and Full IQs; the WISC—Verbal, Performance, and Full IQs; the short version of the WISC; Rutter's behavior "B" scale for teachers; a teachers' questionnaire designed for this study, which explored children's school adjustment and behavior; a review of school records; and information on the job status of the older subjects.

School-aged subjects were tested in their classrooms. Each A subject and a corresponding biological family subject who was nearest to the A child in age were tested. The entire classes of these subjects took the ECNI. A and B subjects were given the full-scale WISC; two others per subject from the subjects' classrooms, matched for social environment (socioeconomic status), were given a short form of the WISC. The teachers of the subjects and of the controls completed the behavior "B" scale and the study's questionnaire. The school testing was done over a period of three years; school records were explored through the 1977–78 school year. Additional follow-up for some of the B and C subjects was done over an additional two years to collect job history information.

Overall, IQ scores were obtained for 94% of the A's, 55% of the B's, and 95% of the C's. An index of scholastic success or failure was calculated for each A, B, and C subject from information derived from the school records. The teachers' "B" scale was completed for all but five of the school-aged children. The teacher's questionnaire was completed for all A and B subjects born after 1960; it included ratings of the degree to which each subject was gifted and of the level of his or her adjustment to school.

Runyan and Gould 1985

The authors of this article were interested in exploring the *iatrogenic* damage (damage resulting from the treatment received) done to child victims of maltreatment who were placed in out-of-home care. Juvenile delinquency was used as the potential marker for this damage. A matched historical cohort design was utilized; the authors compared the rate of subsequent juvenile delinquency between children currently in out-of-home care because they had been maltreated and children who were maltreated and left in their own homes.

The potential subjects were children who have been maltreated in six central North Carolina counties. *Maltreatment* was defined as the presence of a confirmed report of neglect or abuse by a parent or guardian in the cumulative social service record. The "treatment" cohort was defined as all children presently in unrelated family foster care who had been in care for at least three consecutive years. It included adolescents who had been in family foster homes for at least three years but who, at the time of data collection, were hospitalized, incarcerated, or in group homes. Excluded were children whose social service or school records indicated that they either were severely mentally retarded or had IQ scores under 50 on either the Stanford-Binet or the Wechsler Intelligence Scale of Children-Revised (WISC-R). In the six counties, 114 children in out-of-home care met the study criteria.

A comparison cohort was formed by systematically searching the records of the county departments of social services for maltreated children who most closely resembled the treatment subjects in terms of the date of report, age, the year in which they were confirmed as maltreated, the perpetrator of their maltreatment, and services provided in the home. Those who moved from the county or who later were placed in out-of-home care were excluded from the group. The comparison cohort contained 106 youth; 69 of them matched a child in out-of-home care by age at report, year of report, gender, and race; 19 matched by all of these factors except gender or race; 19 were selected by allowing the year of report to vary while matching for the child's current age. (While the comparison cohort was said to number 106, these figures inexplicably add up to 107.) The other eight foster children could not be matched owing to the inadequacy of the social service records. Because an earlier North Carolina study found that the type or severity of maltreatment bore little relation to the decision to place the child in care, no attempt was made to match the children by these maltreatment characteristics.

Data were collected by abstracting the cumulative files maintained by social service agencies, juvenile courts, and schools. The types of information collected included type of maltreatment(s) and the age of child at occurrence; type of social services provided by the county agencies; type, duration, and number of foster home placements; race, education, occupation, and marital status of the biological parent(s); observations of behavior by social service agency employees; nature, date, and outcome of all juvenile court hearings; and evidence of severe mental retardation.

Estimates of risk for delinquency were calculated for both of the groups by using an incidence-density measure: the risk of delinquency per year after the child's 11th birthday. This ratio was used to measure the relative risk of juvenile delinquency among children in out-of-home care compared with their peers cared for in their own homes.

At the time of the study, the average age of both the out-of-home care subjects and the home care group was 14.1 years. Sixty-six percent of the foster group and 55% of the home care group were African American; the other subjects were Caucasian. Females comprised 48% of the youth in care and 54% of those staying at home. There was a significant difference between the two groups in the percentage of youth who had experienced physical abuse: 9% of the out-of-home care cohort and 22% of the home care cohort (Student's *t*-test, $p < .05$). They also differed in the percentage that had a history of prior maltreatment: 25% of those in care and 9% of those not removed from their homes (Student's *t*-test, $p < .05$).

Participants who were in out-of-home care had been placed in an average of 2.6 foster homes (median of 2); on average, 8.6 years had passed since the initial report of maltreatment. Thirty-two percent of the subjects had had only one placement, while 20% had had four or more; two had been in nine foster homes and one had been in 11. The mean duration of the first home placement was 3.6 years.

Records of 77 of the 106 home care participants were complete enough to yield accurate information regarding the services they received in the home. The average number of visits by workers in the first two months was 5.3, and the mean number of visits by six months was 8.25. Home services were provided for an average of 22 months ($N = 60$).

Quinton, Rutter, and Liddle 1986

This prospective follow-up study explored the questions of whether there is a continuity between adverse experiences in childhood and poor parenting behavior in adult life. Related questions included how to interpret such a connection if it exists, how to explain the adequate functioning of some people who had disadvantaged backgrounds, and whether there are modifiable or reversible effects of adverse childhood experiences.

The methodology of this project combined retrospective and prospective research strategies to explore intergenerational links. On the retrospective side, admission into care was treated as the dependent variable; the question asked was how often the parenting problems shown by these adults were associated with their experiences of adverse parenting themselves when they were children. A prospective approach was used, in which admission into care was treated as an independent variable, to determine the likelihood that the experience of poor parenting in childhood would lead to parenting difficulties in the same individual when she was an adult.

The authors studied two groups of British women who had first been studied in the mid-1960s when they were children (Rutter [1967]). The first group comprised 94 girls who, in 1964, had been residents in one of two Children's Homes run as group cottages; they had been admitted because of a breakdown in parenting. Data from past studies with this sample were available to the current researchers; they included information regarding the girls' behavior at school and about the regimens of the cottages. The current sample was restricted to subjects who had been identified as "white" and who were 21 to 27 years old on January 1, 1978. Of the original 94 "ex-care" females, five had died by the time of follow-up. Eighty-one of the remaining 89 subjects (91%) were interviewed, including one living in Germany and three living in Australia.

The comparison group consisted of young women who had also served as controls in a 1981 study by Quinton and Rutter. They had originally been selected because they were in the same school classes as children of mentally ill parents; according to the authors, this selection process did not seem to introduce relevant distortions or biases. These young women were the same age as the ex-care subjects, never had been admitted into care, were living with their families in the same general area in inner London, and had had their school behavior assessed at approximately the same age as the other cohort by means of the same questionnaire. They were followed to the ages of 21 to 27 in the same way as the ex-care subjects. Of the original 51 controls, 41 (80%) were interviewed; five refused to participate, and five could not be located.

Data were collected through interviews with subjects and their spouses, using a nonschedule standardized approach. Topics covered included childhood experiences; family, peer, and work experiences in later life; current circumstance and functioning and adjustment; parenting skills (assessed through responses in dealing with issues of control, peer relations, and distress); and the amount and nature of parental involvement in play. Summary ratings were assigned on the overall style of parenting, effectiveness and consistency of control, parental sensitivity to the child's needs, and the amounts of expressed warmth toward and criticism of the child. In addition, direct home observations were made of interactions between the mothers and their children ages two to three and one-half.

The parenting index chosen for this study was the admission of a child into the care of a local authority because the parent was no longer able to cope with the task of child rearing. This index was selected because it met the following criteria: (1) it reflected severe and persistent parenting difficulties; (2) the difficulties it reflected were reasonably common in the general population; (3) the difficulties it reflected were known to increase substantially the risk that children will develop disorders of psychosocial development; and (4) the index was capable of being employed on an epidemiological basis both to identify families currently experiencing parenting difficulties and to identify individuals who have experienced similar problems as children.

Barth 1990

Targeted youth in the San Francisco Bay Area and Sacramento included those who were at least 16 years old at the time of emancipation from out-of-home care. Youth who had been placed primarily in juvenile justice or mental health care or who were not emancipated as dependents were excluded.

The sample for this study, which contained 55 young adults, is described by the author as "very accidental in composition" (p. 423). The study employed multiple strategies, including posting flyers in public agencies, payment for interviews, and contacting foster parents, group care providers, social workers, and personal contacts, to identify 85 names of youths formerly in care who had left care between 1 and 10 years before. Almost 25% could not be reached.

The average age of the contacted youth was 21 years. The mean ages at entry into and exit from out-of-home care were 12 and 17.6 years respectively. The majority were Caucasian (72%), with 13% African American and 9% Latino. The typical youth in the study had been out of care for three years.

Data collection involved interviews, typically in the subjects' homes and lasting one to three hours; 24% were by telephone. The interview schedule was designed to describe the experiences of children formerly in care across several life domains, including employment experiences, continued contact with former foster parents and biological relatives, educational preparation, life skills preparation received during care, health and health care use, substance use, criminal activity, and housing and income. Questions also ascertained their satisfaction with out-of-home care and suggestions for youths in care and social workers regarding preparation for independent living.

Fanshel, Finch, and Grundy 1990

Foster Children in a Life Course Perspective is a study of the experiences of 585 adults who as children had been placed for part of their time in care with the Casey Family Program. All persons who had been in the care of Casey homes—some as early as 1966—and discharged by December 31, 1984, were included in the projects. The homes were located in five states: Washington, Idaho, Montana, California, and Oregon. A content analysis of case records was completed for all 585 subjects in the following areas: living arrangements since birth, factors leading to placement, and the adjustment of children at entry, during placement, and at discharge.

The study included a subset of 106 subjects who were interviewed regarding their personal and social functioning. They all lived in one of two communities in Washington—Seattle or Yakima—and had been out of the care of the Casey Family Program for an average of seven years. Forty-five of the people interviewed (42%) were women and 61 (58%) were men.

The authors described the average child placed with the Casey Family Program as being older than the typical foster child and unlikely to be adopted or reunified with the biological family. Most had been permanently separated from their mothers and fathers for a variety of reasons. Many had experienced multiple placements before their admission to Casey and had several placements after Casey as well. As a result, these children were considered at high risk of having developed dysfunctional psychological coping strategies.

Cook, Fleishman, and Grimes 1991

This study was completed by Westat, Inc. under a contract with the Department of Health and Human Services, Administration for Children Youth and Families to evaluate the influence of the Independent Living Initiatives, Public Law 99–272 on (1) states' development of programs, policies, and services; and (2) the impact of services on outcomes for older youths discharged from out-of-home care. The second phase is the most relevant and the focus of this review.

The sample design employed a multistage, stratified design with probability sampling at each of three stages of selection—state, county clusters, and youths 16 and older who were discharged from foster care. During Phase 1 (1988), case record data were obtained from a sample of 1,644 adolescents (weighted to represent 34,600 youth) discharged from care between January 1987 and July 1988. Phase II involved locating these youths 2.5 to 4 years after their discharge. Interviews were conducted with 810 youths between November 1990 and March 1991 to obtain information about their adaptation after leaving the out-of-home care system.

Regression modeling techniques were used to assess the impact of receiving independent living skills training on eight different outcomes: able to maintain a job at least one year; high school graduate; able to access health care when needed; not a cost to the community (e.g., not on welfare, in jail, or on Medicaid); avoided young parenthood; has at least one important person in his or her life; generally very happy with life; and overall success, based on the sum of the other seven measures. The study findings also describe 29 other related outcomes that were assessed for those formerly in out-of-home care, regardless of their receipt of skills training.

While the main focus of this study was on the operationalization and measurement of independent living services, numerous other factors are included as independent variables in the multivariate regression models tested by the researchers. These additional variables are related to demographic characteristics of the youths, characteristics of their out-of-home care experience, and factors that determined their entry into care.

The wide range of variables considered in this study and the sophisticated analytic approach make it a rich data source on the adult functioning of those formerly in care as children. While no direct comparison group is included in the study, the authors provide comparisons with youths in the general and poverty populations for numerous outcomes. The major flaw in the study arises from the inability to locate and interview over half of the original sample discharged from care.

Cook 1992

This doctoral dissertation used the 1988 National Survey of Families and Households to examine the long-term consequences of out-of-home care for adult well-being. The study compared 107 adults formerly in care as children and 12,910 other adults. While the comparison with the nonfoster subjects might be considered like a general population comparison, the author does employ multiple regression techniques to control for demographic and socioeconomic variables (age, race, gender, educational level, marital status, father's and mother's educational level, father's occupational status, and household income). A second stage of the analysis was restricted to care subjects and looked at the contribution of five independent variables related to placement as predictors of adult well-being (age at first placement, number of disruptions, length of time in care, contact with biological parents, and reasons for initial placement). Seven dependent variables were used: life happiness, depression, self-esteem, marital happiness, paternal relationship, maternal relationship, and social isolation.

Appendix C

Studies of Homelessness and Out-of-Home Care

STUDY	TYPE OF STUDY	CHARACTERISTICS OF SAMPLE
Crystal, S. (1984). Homeless men and homeless women: The gender gap. *Urban and Social Change Review, 17*(2), 2–6.	Cross-sectional	N = 8,051 for intake assessment study Ages: 67% < 40 Gender: Intakes: 77.7% male, 22.3% female Race: Not reported Selection criteria: Admission into a New York City shelter between Nov. 1, 1982, and Dec. 31, 1983.
Susser, E., Struening, E., & Conover, S. (1987). Childhood experiences of homeless men. *American Journal of Psychiatry, 144*(12), 1589–1601.	Cross-sectional	N = 918 (223 male first-time users of shelters and 695 male longer-term shelter residents) Ages: Over 70% were under 40 Race: Over 70% were members of ethnic or racial minority groups Selection criteria: Men using New York City's municipal shelters for single adults. For longer-term residents, a weighted representative sample of shelter residents was chosen. The first-timers were interviewed as they entered the shelter for the first time.

Data Collection	Response Rate	Out-of-Home Care Information
1982 to 1983. Intake instrument used for psychosocial assessments in most NYC shelters; intakes took place soon after admission.	Not reported	Intakes: 7.4% of women and 2.8% of men had lived primarily in Out-of-Home care settings or institutional settings as children; more (percentage unreported) had been in such settings for short amounts of time.
Spring and summer 1985. 52-page interview lasting on average 80 minutes.	Not reported	Before the age of 17, 17% of longer-term homeless and 23% of "first-timers" had been placed in out-of-home care. There was an association between childhood placement and history of psychiatric hospitalization ($p < .001$) for both first-timers and longer-term residents.

STUDY	TYPE OF STUDY	CHARACTERISTICS OF SAMPLE
Sosin, M., Colson, P., & Grossman, S. (1988). *Homelessness in Chicago: Poverty and pathology, social institutions, and social change.* Chicago: University of Chicago, School of Social Service Administration.	Longitudinal	N = 536 from free-meal programs in Chicago (34% homeless, 66% domiciled) Ages: 66% £ 40 Gender: 70% male, 30% female Race: 69% African American, 19% Caucasian, 9% Latino, 2% other Selection criteria: Individuals staying in shelters; on streets; short, nonpaying stays with friends or relatives; and those in treatment centers with no-where to go later.
Susser, E., Lin, S., Conover, S., & Struening, E. (1991). Childhood antecedents of homelessness in psychiatric patients. *American Journal of Psychiatry, 148,* 1026–1030.	Cross-sectional	N = 783 (three groups of homeless psychiatric patients in New York City, totaling 512; and 271 never-homeless psy-chiatric patients, also from New York City). Ages: Homeless patients: 64% < 40; never-homeless patients: 73% < 40. Gender: Homeless patients: 85% male; never-homeless patients: 62% male Race: Homeless patients: 55% African American, 45% other; never-homeless patients: 51% African American, 49% other Selection criteria: Inpatient status; homelessness defined as sleeping in shelters or pub-lic places from age 17 onward.

Data Collection	Reponse Rate	Out-of-Home Care Information
1986. Interviews of approximately 45 min. to 1 hour; subjects paid $5.	81%	Homeless adults: 14.5% experienced out-of-home care; domiciled adults: 7.2% experienced out-of-home care.
Data collected for first sample in 1985; second sample in 1987, third sample and never homeless in 1988 to 1989.	Not reported for shelter samples; 96% for Bellevue; 86% for state hospital	Homeless sample: > 15% experienced family foster care; > 10% experienced group home placement; Never-homeless sample: 2% experienced family foster care; 1% experienced group-home placement.

STUDY	TYPE OF STUDY	CHARACTERISTICS OF SAMPLE
Sosin, M., Piliavin, I., & Westerfelt, H. (1990). Toward a longitudinal analysis of homelessness. *Journal of Social Issues, 46*(4), 157–174.	Longitudinal	2 samples interviewed twice, six months apart (A and B) (A) cross-section N = 338 first interview N = 200 second interview Ages: 32.3 (mean) Gender: 85% male Race: 43% Caucasian, 26% African American, 23% Native American, 8% other Selection criteria: homeless adults in Minneapolis, located through community agencies. Homeless = (1) staying at least 1 day but less than 7 days with friend or relative, aware situation was temporary; (2) living in selected boarding-house less than 7 days, rent paid by welfare agency; (3) sleeping in temporary, free shelter; or (4) spent prior night in abandoned building, car, alley, doorway. (B) Recent arrivals N = 113 first interview N = 65 second interview Ages: 31.3 (mean) Gender: 77% male Race: 48% Caucasian, 25% African American, 22% Native American, 5% other Selection criteria: same as above with additional criterion of being homeless this time for less than 14 days.

Data Collection	Reponse Rate	Out-of-Home Care Information
1985-1986. Series of two 45-minute interviews: from 11/85 to 3/86, and from 4/86 to 5/86. Subjects were paid for their time.	Response rate >90%. Population hard to track. 41% attrition rate between rounds 1 & 2 for cross-sectional sample; 42% for recent-arrivals sample.	39% of cross-section had received some form of out-of-home care as children; 35% of the recent arrivals had.

STUDY	TYPE OF STUDY	CHARACTERISTICS OF SAMPLE
Mangine, S., Royse, D., Weihe, V., & Nietzel, M. (1990). Homelessness among adults raised as foster children: A survey of drop-in center users. *Psychological Reports, 67,* 739–745.	Cross-sectional	N = 74 Ages: 36 (mean) Gender: 90% male Race: 70% Caucasian, 28% African American Selection criteria: Subjects chosen from drop-in center and soup kitchen.

DATA COLLECTION	REPONSE RATE	OUT-OF-HOME CARE INFORMATION
Winter and spring 1988.	Not reported	16% reported that they had been a ward of the state prior to age 18.

References

References

Allerhand, M. E., Weber, R. E., & Haug, M. (1966). *Adaptation and adaptability: The Bellefaire follow-up study.* New York: Child Welfare League of America.

Barth, R. P. (1990). On their own: The experiences of youth after foster care. *Child and Adolescent Social Work, 7*(5), 419–40.

Barth, R. P., & Berry, M. (1987). Outcomes of child welfare services under permanency planning. *Social Service Review, 61,* 71–90.

Barth, R. P., & Berry, M. (1988). *Adoption and disruption: Rates, risks, and responses.* New York: Aldine de Gruyter.

Blumstein, A., Cohen, J., Roth, J. A., & Visher, C. A. (1986). *Criminal careers and "career criminals"* (vol. 1). Washington, DC: National Academy Press.

Cook, R., Fleishman, E., & Grimes, V. (1991). *A national evaluation of Title IV-E foster care independent living programs for youth: Phase 2, final report* (vol. 1) (unpublished report. Westat, Inc., Rockville, MD).

Cook, S. K. (1992). *Long term consequences of foster care for adult well-being* (unpublished doctoral dissertation, University of Nebraska, Lincoln).

Costin, L. B., Bell, C. J., & Downs, S. (1991). *Child welfare policies and practice.* New York: Longman.

Crystal. S. (1984). Homeless men and homeless women: The gender gap. *Urban and Social Change Review, 17*(2), 2–6.

Demchak, T. (1985, September/October). Out of foster care, into the streets: Services ordered for homeless youth. *Youth Law News, 6*, 12–15.

Dumaret, A. (1985). IQ, scholastic performance, and behaviors of sibs raised in contrasting environments. *Journal of Child Psychology and Psychiatry and Allied Disciplines, 26*(4), 553–80.

Fanshel, D., Finch, S. J., & Grundy, J. F. (1989). Foster children in life-course perspective: The Casey Family Program experience. *Child Welfare, 68*(5), 467–78.

Fanshel, D., Finch, S. J., & Grundy, J. F. (1990). *Foster children in a life-course perspective*. New York: Columbia University.

Fanshel, D., & Shinn, E. B. (1978). *Children in foster care: A longitudinal investigation*. New York: Columbia University.

Ferguson, T. (1966). *Children in care—and after*. London: Oxford University Press.

Festinger, T. (1983). *No one ever asked us...A postscript to foster care*. New York: Columbia University.

Fischer, J. (1976). *The effectiveness of social casework*. Springfield, IL: Thomas.

Fox, M., and Arcuri, K. (1980). Cognitive and academic functioning in foster children. *Child Welfare, 59*, 491–96.

Frommer, E. A., & O'Shea, G. (1973a). Antenatal identification of women liable to have problems in managing their infants. *British Journal of Psychiatry, 123*, 149–56.

Frommer, E. A., & O'Shea, G. (1973b). The importance of childhood experience in relation to problems of marriage and family-building. *British Journal of Psychiatry, 123*, 157–60.

Frost, S., and Jurich, A. P. (1983). *Follow-up study of children residing in The Villages* (unpublished report, The Villages, Topeka, KS).

Gershenson, C. (1993). Personal communication.

Harari, T. (1980). *Teenagers exiting from foster family care: A retrospective look* (unpublished doctoral dissertation, University of California, Berkeley).

Heston, L. L., Denney, D. D., & Pauly, I. B. (1966). The adult adjustment of persons institutionalized as children. *British Journal of Psychiatry, 112*, 1103–1110.

Izzo, R. L., & Ross, R. R. (1990). Meta-analysis of rehabilitation programs for juvenile delinquents: A brief report. *Criminal Justice and Behavior, 17*(1), 134–142.

Jones, M. A., & Moses, B. (1984). *West Virginia's former foster children: Their experiences in care and their lives as young adults.* New York: Child Welfare League of America.

Kadushin, A. (1974). *Child welfare services* (2nd ed.). New York: Macmillan.

Kadushin, A., & Martin, J. A. (1988). *Child welfare services* (4th ed.). New York: Macmillan.

Kleine, D. (1990). Anxiety and sport performance: A meta-analysis. *Anxiety Research, 2*(2), 113–131.

Kraus, J. (1981). Foster children grown up: Parameters of care and adult delinquency. *Children and Youth Services Review, 3,* 99–114.

Laird, J., & Hartman, A. (1985). *A handbook of child welfare: Context, knowledge, and practice.* New York: The Free Press.

Light, R. J., & Pillemer, D. B. (1984). *Summing up: The science of reviewing research.* Cambridge: Harvard University Press.

Lindsey, D. (1992). Reliability of the foster care placement decision: A review. *Research in Social Work Practice, 2*(1), 65–80.

Lindsey, D. (1994). The welfare of children (unpublished manuscript, New York: Oxford University Press).

Maas, H. S. (1963). The young adult adjustment of twenty wartime residential nursery children. *Child Welfare, 42,* 57–72.

Maas, H. S. (1969). Children in long term foster care. *Child Welfare, 48*(6), 321–333, 347.

Maas, H., & Engler, R. (1959). *Children in need of parents.* New York: Columbia University Press.

Maluccio, A. N., Fein, E., & Olmstead, K. A. (1986). *Permanency planning for children: Concepts and methods.* New York: Tavistock Publications.

Mangine, S., Royse, D., Wiehe, V., and Nietzel, M. (1990). Homelessness among adults raised as foster children: A survey of drop-in center users. *Psychological Reports, 67,* 739–745.

McCord, J., McCord, W., & Thurber, E. (1960). The effects of foster-home placement in the prevention of adult antisocial behavior. *Social Service Review, 34,* 415–419.

McDonald, T. P., Lieberman, A., Poertner, J., & Hornby, H. (1989). Child welfare standards for success. *Children and Youth Services Review, 11,* 319–330.

Mech, E. (1970). Decision analysis in foster care practice. In H. D. Stone (Ed.), *Foster care in question* (pp. 26–51). New York: Child Welfare League of America.

Meier, E. G. (1965). Current circumstances of former foster children. *Child Welfare, 44,* 196–206.

National Opinion Research Center. (1978). *General social surveys, 1972–78.* Ann Arbor, MI: The Inter-University Consortium for Political and Social Research.

Nelson, K. (1990). How do we know that family-based services are effective? *The Prevention Report,* Fall, 1–3.

Newman, E., & Turem, J. (1974). The crisis of accountability. *Social Work, 10,* 5–17.

Packman, J., Randall, J., & Jacques, N. (1986). *Who needs care? Social work decisions about children.* Oxford: Basil Blackwell.

Palmer, S. E. (1976). *Children in long term care: Their experience and progress.* Canada: Family and Children's Services of London and Middlesex.

Piliavin, I., & Sosin, M. (1988). Longitudinal study of the homeless. Unpublished manuscript. Summarized in *Focus* [newsletter of the Institute for Research on Poverty, University of Wisconsin-Madison], *10*(4), 20–24.

Piliavin, I., Sosin, M. & Westerfelt, H. (1987). Conditions contributing to long-term homelessness: An exploration study. Discussion Paper no. 853–87, Institute for Research on Poverty, University of Wisconsin-Madison.

Quinton, D., Rutter, M., & Liddle, C. (1986). Institutional rearing, parenting difficulties, and marital support. In S. Chess & A. Thomas (Eds.), *Annual progress in child psychiatry and child development,* 1985, (pp. 173–206). New York: Brunner/ Mazel.

Rest, E. R., & Watson, K. W. (1984). Growing up in foster care. *Child Welfare, 63*(4), 291–306.

Robins, L. N. (1966). *Deviant children grown up: A sociological and psychiatric study of sociopathic personality.* Baltimore: Williams and Wilkins.

Royse, D., & Wiehe, V. R. (1989). Assessing effects of foster care on adults raised as foster children: A methodological issue. *Psychological Reports, 64,* 671–78.

Runyan, D. K., & Gould, C. (1985). Foster care for child maltreatment: Impact on delinquent behavior. *Pediatrics, 75,* 562–68.

Rutter, M. (1967). A children's behaviour questionnaire by teachers: Preliminary findings. *Journal of Child Psychology and Psychiatry, 8*(1–11).

Rzepnicki, T. L. (1987). Recidivism of foster children returned to their own homes: A review and new directions for research. *Social Service Review, 61*(1), 56–70.

Sosin, M., Colson, P., & Grossman, S. (1988). *Homelessness in Chicago: Poverty and pathology, social institutions, and social change.* Chicago: University of Chicago, School of Social Service Administration.

Sosin, M., Piliavin, I., & Westerfelt, H. (1990). Toward a longitudinal analysis of homelessness. *Journal of Social Issues, 46*(4), 157–174.

Statistical Abstract of the United States (SAUS). (1967, 1980, 1982, 1983, 1984, 1985, 1986, 1991). Washington, DC: U.S. Government Printing Office.

Susser, E., Lin, S., Conover, S., & Struening, E. (1991). Childhood antecedents of homelessness in psychiatric patients. *American Journal of Psychiatry, 148,* 1026–1030.

Susser, E., Struening, E. L., & Conover, S. (1987). Childhood experiences of homeless men. *American Journal of Psychiatry, 144*(12), 1599–1601.

Theis, S. (1924). *How foster children turn out.* New York: State Charities Aid Association.

Triseliotis, J. (1980). Growing up in foster care and after. In J. Triseliotis (Ed.), *New developments in foster care and adoption* (pp. 131–61). London: Routledge and Kegan Paul.

Triseliotis, J., & Russell, J. (1984). *Hard to place: The outcome of adoption and residential care.* London: Heinemann Educational Books.

Trotzkey, E. (1930). *Institutional care and placing-out.* Chicago: Marks Nathan Jewish Orphan Home.

U.S. Bureau of the Census. (1980a). *Census of population (Illinois).* General social and economic characteristics. Washington, DC: U.S. Government Printing Office.

U.S. Bureau of the Census. (1980b). *Census of population (Kansas).* General social and economic characteristics. Washington, DC: U.S. Government Printing Office.

U.S. Bureau of the Census. (1980c). *Census of population (Louisiana).* General social and economic characteristics. Washington, DC: U.S. Government Printing Office.

U.S. Bureau of the Census. (1980d). *Census of population (New York)*. General social and economic characteristics. Washington, DC: U.S. Government Printing Office.

U.S. Bureau of the Census. (1980e). *Census of population (West Virginia)*. General social and economic characteristics. Washington, DC: U.S. Government Printing Office.

U.S. Bureau of the Census. (1983). *Census of population (California)*. General social and economic characteristics. Washington, DC: U.S. Government Printing Office.

U.S. Bureau of the Census. (1990). Current Population Reports. *What is it worth?* Household Economic Studies, Series P-70, No. 221.

U.S. House of Representatives, Select Committee on Children, Youth, and Families. (1989). *No place to call home: Discarded children in America*. Washington, DC: U.S. Government Printing Office.

Wald, M. S., Carlsmith, J. M., & Leiderman, P. H. (1988). *Protecting abused and neglected children*. Stanford, CA: Stanford University Press.

Wolins, M., & Piliavin, I. (1964). Child maltreatment and maternal deprivation among AFDC recipient families. *Social Service Review, 53*, 175–94.

Wolkind, S. N. (1977a). A child's relationships after admission to residential care. *Child Care, Health, and Development, 3*, 357–62.

Wolkind, S. N. (1977b). Women who have been "in care"—psychological and social status during pregnancy. *Journal of Child Psychology and Psychiatry, 18*, 179–82.

Yuan, Y. T. (1990). *Evaluation of AB 1562 in-home care demonstration projects, Vol. I: Final report*. Sacramento, CA: Walter R. McDonald & Associates, Inc.

Zimmerman, R. B. (1982). Foster care in retrospect. *Tulane Studies in Social Welfare, 14*.

About the Authors

Thomas P. McDonald received his Ph.D. from the University of Wisconsin. He is currently Professor at the University of Kansas, School of Social Welfare, where he is conducting research on caregiving in families with children with serious emotional disorders, on adoption services, and on placement prevention. He has worked on numerous projects with state child welfare agencies.

Reva I. Allen received her M.A. from the University of Chicago. She is Research Associate at the University of Kansas, School of Social Welfare, currently working on her doctorate. She is secretary of the National Association of Social Workers board of directors. Her work focuses on the needs of children and families and how to assess and increase the family centeredness of mental health services.

Alex Westerfelt received his Ph.D. from the University of Wisconsin-Madison. He is Assistant Professor at the University of Kansas, School of Social Welfare, where he is conducting research on adults and children who are homeless. He has been a child welfare worker in both the public and private sector.

231

Irving Piliavin received his D.S.W. from Columbia University. He is currently Professor Emeritus at the School of Social Work, University of Wisconsin-Madison, and is a faculty affiliate for the Institute for Research on Poverty. He is engaged in research on children aging out of out-of-home care and research evaluating the impact of welfare reform.